freshwater fish
of the northeast

Illustrated by MATT PATTERSON

Text by DAVID A. PATTERSON

University Press of New England

Hanover and London

freshwater
fish *of the*
northeast

UNIVERSITY PRESS OF NEW ENGLAND

One Court Street, Lebanon NH 03766

www.upne.com

© 2010 University Press of New England

All rights reserved

Printed in China

Designed and typeset in Miller and Didot
by Eric M. Brooks

For permission to reproduce any of the
material in this book, contact Permissions,
University Press of New England,
One Court Street, Lebanon NH 03766;
or visit www.upne.com

5 4 3 2 1

Library of Congress
Cataloging-in-Publication Data
Patterson, Matt.
Freshwater fish of the Northeast / illustrated by
Matt Patterson; text by David A. Patterson.
    p. cm.
Includes bibliographical references.
ISBN 978-1-58465-819-1 (cloth: alk. paper)
1. Freshwater fishes—Northeastern States.
2. Freshwater fishes—Northeastern States—
Pictorial works. I. Patterson, David A., 1949–
II. Title.
QL628.N92P38   2010
597.0974—dc22   2009044794

This book is dedicated to
Alexander "Syd" Patterson:
my dad, Matt's grandfather,
and Brody's great-grandfather.
Four generations of fishing
started with him. Thanks for
taking me fishing, Dad.

Contents

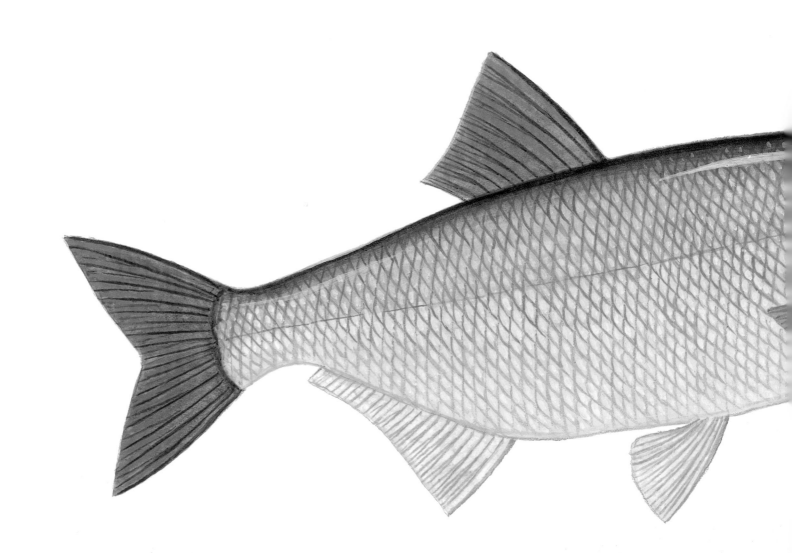

Introduction

Most of us go fishing for the thrill of catching a gamefish. Along the way, we catch other species of fish that may not be particularly edible nor the reason we hiked down to the river. Nonetheless, they are an integral part of the fishing experience. This book is an acknowledgment and a celebration not only of the freshwater gamefish but also of the other fish that you catch when you are out there fishing. Note that shad and striped bass are anadromous fish, but have not become landlocked in freshwater (in the Northeast). We have included only fish that spend their entire lives in freshwater, even if it is by becoming landlocked.

In the process of writing and illustrating this book, my son Matt (the illustrator) and I decided to have a species contest. The object of the contest is to catch as many different species of freshwater fish as we can over the course of the summer. The winner will enjoy a fish dinner at the expense of the loser. We photograph and identify each fish, and record its name in a journal. The contest has motivated us to take trips beyond our usual fishing haunts and forced us to try different fishing methods and a variety of baits. We have a catch, photograph, and release policy: After we photograph the fish, we immediately set them free. The whole process has been a great deal of fun and it is surprising how fast the numbers of species add up. Our attempt to capture every fish illustrated in this book is an ongoing project that we look forward to pursuing. It may take us years, but we'll be enjoying ourselves and learning more through the process.

During my thirty-four years as a biology teacher, I often collected wild fish from local ponds and rivers. I placed them in the many freshwater aquariums in my classrooms, complete with broken beer bottles and cans as hiding places for the crayfish and smaller fish. The various sunfish, small bass, and the occasional less common fish swam around the tanks and stared out at my students. I found it was much easier to relate my subject matter to wild local fish, rather than to exotic species from some far-off part of the world. Some fish species did better in the aquariums than others. The fish that did well would donate about seven months of their lives to science. At the end of the school year, we would return the fish to the same pond or river where they were collected.

Teaching biology encompasses more than just fish, but I tried to incorporate fish into my lessons whenever possible. An important part of the ecosystem, fish can be included in discussions on many biological topics, such as ecology, predator/prey relationships, protective coloration, diffusion and osmosis, classification, and vertebrate anatomy and physiology. And, as I always told my students, my fish came from only the finest schools.

Matt has been painting animals since his preschool days. It was obvious from the beginning that he had an aptitude for drawing and a keen interest in all manner of wildlife. He has spent much of his young life combining these two interests. Over the years, Matt has won a number of art contests, including being named "Best of Show" in the New Hampshire Federal Junior Duck Stamp Competition three years in a row and placing in the top ten nationally. His beautiful fish illustrations were rendered first in pencil and then completed with acrylic paints. Most of the illustrations in this book are based on our photographs of actual live catches, while a few relied on available reference and photographic sources. As a professional illustrator, Matt has illustrated a wide range of wildlife beyond the fish in this book and I'm sure you'll be seeing more of his work in the future.

Working on this book has been a unique joy for both of us, combining my lifelong interest in biology with my son's artistic talents. We hope that the paintings will convey the beauty and diversity that inspire our love of the outdoors and perhaps move you to take greater notice of the wonders that abound in our region's rivers, lakes, and streams.

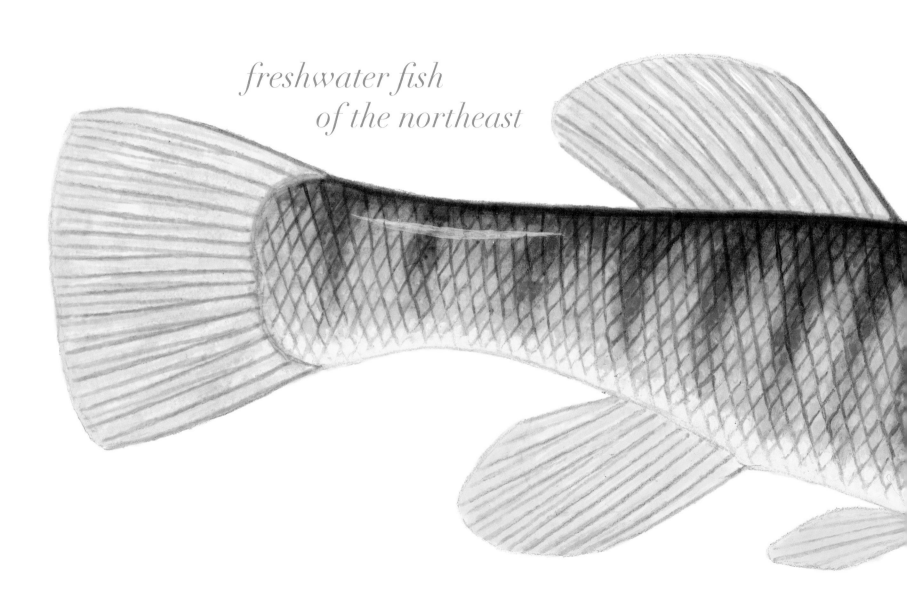

freshwater fish
of the northeast

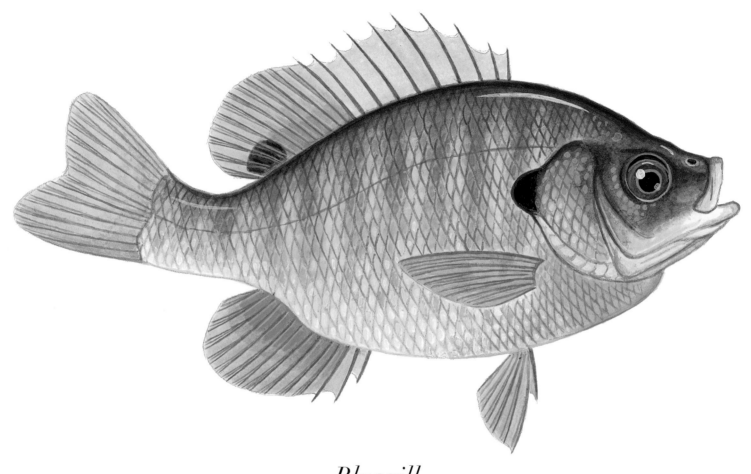

Bluegill

LEPOMIS MACROCHIRUS

5–8 inches

Bluegill coloration can vary, but generally they are greenish brown, with vertical bars on their sides. They have a black flap on the posterior end of their operculum (gill cover). Bluegill have a distinctive black blotch on the posterior soft part of their double, joined dorsal fin. This black blotch is the best way to identify bluegill, because other species of sunfish do not have this marking. Spawning males may have an orange or reddish belly.

Bluegill are common in clean, warm-water ponds and rivers in the Northeast and around the United States. They usually are grouped with a number of species referred to as sunfish. Large bluegill sometimes venture out beyond the weeds into deeper water where there is less competition for food; however, most individuals inhabit the shallower water near a pond's edge. They like to hide among lily pads, under fallen trees and logs, by submerged rocks, or near other floating or sunken debris.

Bluegill can be caught using many fishing methods. Their small mouths point upward, indicating that they are largely surface feeders. Using light tackle is best, as they can put up quite a fight for their size. Fly-fishing might be the most exciting method of catching these aggressive fighters, but most small live baits will work as well, with worms leading the list. Some anglers use live grasshoppers or crickets. They are a great "starter fish" for children—all you need is a bobber and a worm and the excitement begins. Bluegill are among the most popular fish to eat in many parts of the country. Most people fillet even the smaller ones.

Pumpkinseed

LEPOMIS GIBBOSUS

5–8 inches

Pumpkinseeds are roughly the same size as bluegill and look similar to bluegill and other sunfish in structure and shape, but differ in coloration. Pumpkinseeds are quite vibrant and distinctive-looking. The dark dorsal surface is brownish green. The sides are often light blue, almost turquoise, with scattered orange spots and sometimes vague, dark bands (somewhat like the bluegill, but not as prominent). The belly is yellow to orange. The operculum has alternating horizontal bands of bronze and blue. The opercular flap is black, with a red rim on the posterior end. This red rim is the best identifying mark for the pumpkinseed. Although longear sunfish sometimes have some red on or around their opercular flaps, the flaps are much longer than the smaller, rounder flaps of pumpkinseeds (longear sunfish also are quite rare in the Northeast and not as likely to be encountered). The pectoral fins of pumpkinseeds and bluegill are longer and more pointed than those of other sunfish in the Northeast.

Pumpkinseeds are a very widespread and plentiful sunfish, common to most ponds, lakes, and slow-moving rivers throughout the Northeast. They range south to Georgia, west to the Mississippi drainage, and have been introduced in other areas. Pumpkinseeds usually frequent the same warm, weedy habitats as bluegill, the other sunfish abundant in the Northeast. They feed on insects and insect larvae as well as on a variety of crustaceans and mollusks.

Pumpkinseeds are another very tasty panfish. They are fun to catch on a fly rod or light spinning tackle. My father-in-law always kept his fly rod leaning on the shed down by the pond. He would catch one pumpkinseed after another using a floating popper. Muffin the cat was often the beneficiary of these catches. Like other sunfish, they are easy for kids to catch using a worm and a bobber.

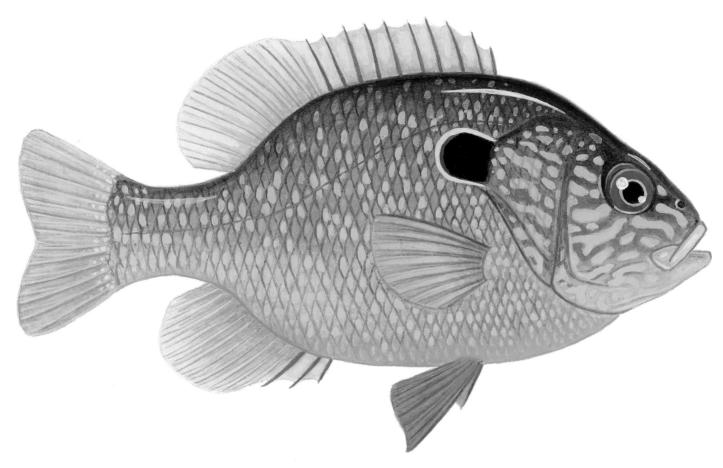

Longear Sunfish

LEPOMIS MEGALOTIS

3–6 inches

Longear sunfish have alternating patches of blue-green and bronze on their sides and a yellow to orange belly. The head has wavy, alternating bands of blue-green and bronze extending through the operculum, making it a very colorful sunfish. Longear and redbreast sunfish both have long, black opercular flaps (the name "longear" comes from the shape of this flap). However, the flaps of longear sunfish are outlined in white, providing the best distinguishing feature. Longear sunfish occasionally have red in their opercular flap, similar to pumpkinseeds. The pectoral fins of longear sunfish are slightly more rounded than those of redbreast sunfish.

Their range extends west through Ontario to Minnesota and south through the Mississippi Basin to the Gulf States, but they are not that common in the Northeast.

Longear sunfish, like many other sunfish, favor warm water, vegetation, and still to slow-moving water. They feed on insects floating on the surface, and small crustaceans, insect larvae, and small fish found deeper in the water. They are an edible panfish, but their smaller size limits their overall interest to anglers. They can be caught easily with small live bait such as worms, as well as with small lures and flies.

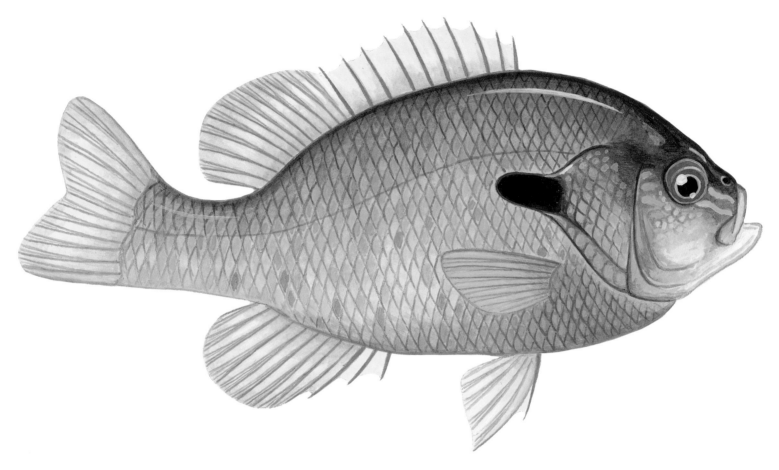

Redbreast Sunfish

LEPOMIS AURITUS

6–8 inches

Redbreast sunfish are named for their brilliant orange-red to red belly. Males tend to be brighter in color than females, especially during breeding season in the early summer. The darker back tapers into lighter sides, with red-orange spots on a bluish background. Redbreast sunfish also have light blue lines in front of and below their eyes. The very long, black opercular flaps resemble those of longear sunfish, but are not outlined in white. Redbreast sunfish have slightly more elongated bodies than many other common sunfish in the genus *Lepomis*.

Redbreast sunfish tend to inhabit slightly deeper water in ponds and lakes than do bluegill and pumpkinseeds. Their range extends from Maine to Florida, west along the Gulf States and into Texas. They are not abundant anywhere in the Northeast, but moderate populations are found here and there.

Redbreasts are widely sought after as a gamefish in some parts of the country, although they are not considered a major sport fish in the Northeast. Nonetheless, they are caught along with other panfish where they exist. Their flaky white meat is considered a delicacy by some. Redbreast sunfish respond nicely to live bait such as worms, crickets, and small minnows, as well as to small spinners, flies, and lures. They can put up a good fight for their size.

Banded Sunfish

ENNEACANTHUS OBESUS

3–4 inches

Banded sunfish are olive-green, sprinkled with small, greenish gold spots on their bodies and fins. They are named for the dark, blackish green, vertical bands on their sides, although bluegill, pumpkinseeds, redbreast sunfish, and longear sunfish all have some sort of dark, vertical lateral bands. However, these bands are most distinctive in banded sunfish. Also, all of these other sunfish have indented caudal fins, while banded sunfish have rounded caudal fins.

Banded sunfish inhabit shallow, weedy ponds and rivers in central New England, particularly Massachusetts. They are found in a few spots in southern New Hampshire and Maine and into Connecticut. They are rare in New York State (although a few populations are found on Long Island), and scarce in Pennsylvania, but have been found here and there in the Eastern coastal states south into Florida. Their exact range is somewhat uncertain because fishermen don't usually catch them and they are not used as baitfish. Most fishermen probably don't realize that this species of sunfish exists. It is possible to catch one on a fishing line but most of the population in a pond may be even smaller than 3 or 4 inches.

I collected a few banded sunfish each year for the freshwater aquariums in my biology classroom so we could compare their characteristics with more common sunfish. They would do very well in the aquariums. At the end of the year, we would release them to the same pond where they were collected.

Rock Bass

AMBLOPLITES RUPESTRIS

6–10 inches

The most distinctive feature of rock bass is their red eyes. Their bodies are dark olive to golden brown, with distinct rows of dark dots forming horizontal stripes on their sides, and light-colored, sometimes almost bluish bellies. Although rock bass are in the sunfish family, their bodies are not as compressed as other sunfish and their mouths are larger, giving them a bass-like appearance. The hinge of the mouth can extend to below the eyes like a bass. They have a dark, triangular teardrop marking below their eyes and a similar dark spot on the end of their operculum. The anterior dorsal fin has eleven or twelve spines, more than most sunfish. The anal fin has five to seven spines.

Rock bass are native to the east-central Mississippi drainage and the Great Lakes. Their range extends into the Northeast, where they have been introduced or have made their way through canal systems such as those entering and connecting the Great Lakes. They are found throughout the Northeast, though they are not common in eastern Massachusetts or Maine. They favor clean lakes, ponds, and slow-moving rivers. As their name indicates, rock bass prefer rocky, boulder-filled bottoms, where they generally feed on aquatic insects, crayfish, and small fish. However, they do occasionally feed on the surface.

They can reach 12 inches in length, but most individuals average about 6 to 10 inches. Many anglers catch rock bass while fishing for smallmouth bass, because they often are found in the same habitats and take the same baits. They will strike readily at spinners, small crank baits, and live bait such as worms, crayfish, and small shiners.

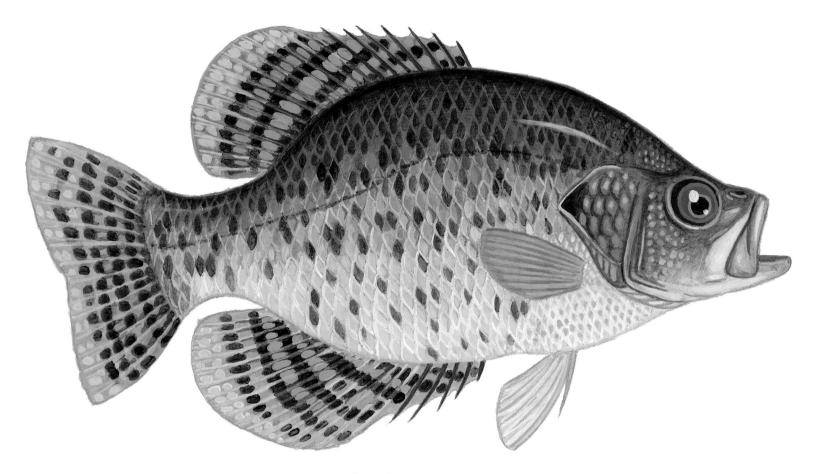

Black Crappie

POMOXIS NIGROMACULATUS

8–12 inches

Black crappie, also known as calico bass, are in the same scientific family as sunfish, with a similar deep body shape; however, they have much larger mouths. Their mouths are very delicate and have very thin skin. Black crappie have a compressed, narrow, greenish silvery body with irregularly shaped black blotches or spots throughout their body and fins. They have a double dorsal fin, joined in the middle, with a spiny anterior and fleshy posterior fin. The posterior dorsal fin is almost a mirror image to the fleshy anal fin, which makes them look much bigger than they actually are when their fins are spread out.

Black crappie most closely resemble white crappie, their closest relative. The names suggest that they can be distinguished easily but black crappie aren't really black, and white crappie have grayish black blotches that form bands on their sides. They have very similarly shaped bodies and fins. However, black crappie have seven or eight spines on their anterior dorsal fins, while white crappie have five or six.

Black crappie are good fighters and are fun to catch on flies, poppers, artificial lures, or spinners. Fishermen also use live bait such as worms and minnows. They are a little more elusive than sunfish, but frequent the same types of lakes and ponds. They become active earlier in the season in the colder Northeast than do bluegill and pumpkinseeds, perhaps because they gather for spawning earlier. Their upward-pointing mouths indicate that they are surface feeders. Take care when removing lures and hooks so as not to damage their large, delicate mouths. Crappie are considered panfish and, like bluegill and other sunfish, they are sought after for their flaky white meat.

White Crappie

POMOXIS ANNULARIS

6–14 inches

White crappie look very much like black crappie, except that they are a bit lighter, with slightly more elongated bodies. White crappie are silvery green to almost yellowish white, with a darker silvery green on the dorsal surface and vertical grayish black bars on the sides. Sometimes the bars are indistinct, but they help distinguish white from black crappie, which have no vertical bars. Another distinction is that white crappie have five or six dorsal spines while black crappie have seven or eight.

The mouths of white crappie are larger than those of bluegill and other sunfish, but they are very delicate and can tear easily. White crappie are quite hardy and tolerate a much wider range of conditions than black crappie, such as murkier water. Both like to hide in vegetation and under logs and brush in the water.

White crappie are in the sunfish family. They are not native to the Northeast, except perhaps in the Great Lakes region. Both species of crappie have been introduced widely over the years, but white crappie are not as widespread as black crappie in the Northeast and not easy to find here.

Spring is the best time to fish for them, because they spawn earlier than bluegill, and will hit almost any bait at that time. Worms, small baitfish, or small spinners will catch white crappie quite easily. They are considered very good eating. They average about three-quarters of a pound but occasionally can reach nearly 5 pounds.

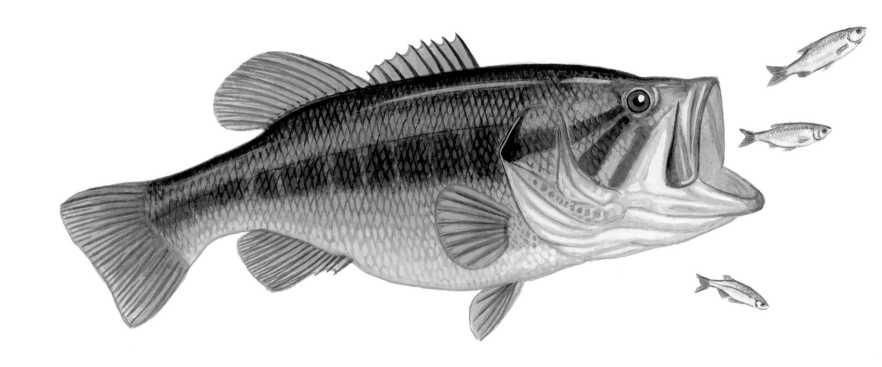

Largemouth Bass

MICROPTERUS SALMOIDES

10–15 inches

Largemouth bass are named for their larger mouths compared to their close relative, the smallmouth bass. The hinge of the mouth extends to behind the eye. The notch between their spiny and fleshy joined dorsal fins is deeper than that of the smallmouth bass, making the two dorsal fins almost separate. Largemouth bass are dark greenish brown on the dorsal surface, a pleasant olive-green on the sides, and white on the belly. The green and white are separated by a wide, dark band running through the operculum and the midline of the body to the tail. This dark band can be patchy and not quite continuous in some individuals.

Largemouth bass grow bigger than smallmouth bass and have a much wider range throughout the United States. They are attracted to warmer bodies of water than smallmouth bass and prefer the weeds and shallows. They are very self-sustaining throughout much of their range, which extends throughout the Northeast and only thins out in the northern extremes of Maine, where the water is colder.

Largemouth bass feed mostly on smaller fish. However, crayfish, insects, insect larvae, frogs, and even small mammals are part of a largemouth bass's diet. They tend to be solitary as adults but may school a bit when they are young. They like clean water, but will survive and even flourish in somewhat murky, warm water.

Largemouth bass are among North America's top gamefish, particularly in the warmer southern states. In the Northeast, they get competition for top gamefish from the various cold-water fish not readily found in the South, such as trout, salmon, walleye, and pike. Live bait, noisy surface plugs, and wobbling underwater lures often bring very good results. Location may be more important than the bait you use. Largemouth bass are very attracted to weeds, submerged logs, and overhangs, where they may attack anything that goes by. They are ferocious fighters and are among the wildest gamefish to reel in. They average 2 to 4 pounds, but individuals sometimes may be taken at 7 or 8 pounds, and occasionally more.

Smallmouth Bass

MICROPTERUS DOLOMIEU

8–14 inches

Smallmouth bass most closely resemble largemouth bass. The names give away the major difference between the two fish: A straight line drawn vertically upward from the outer edge of the hinge of the jaw of a smallmouth bass will pass in front of the eye or slightly through it; in a largemouth bass, it would pass behind the eye. Another distinguishing characteristic is the notch between the two joined dorsal fins: On a smallmouth bass, the notch is not as pronounced as that on the largemouth bass, making the two dorsal fins more joined. Smallmouth bass are olive-green, with dark, vertical bars on their sides. They may be slightly darker green on the dorsal surface, and a bronze color sometimes seems to radiate through the green. The belly is light to almost white. The bars are somewhat irregular and begin on the dorsal surface and go down almost to the belly. Three more bars radiate from the eyes through the operculum.

Smallmouth bass are found throughout the Northeast in gravel- and rocky-bottomed rivers, lakes, and ponds. Despite being an introduced species, they are somewhat self-sustaining throughout most of their range. They are not as widespread as the largemouth bass.

In the spring and early summer, smallmouth bass will charge out from the protection of a large boulder or submerged log at almost any artificial bass lure. They seek cooler, deeper water in the summer. Crayfish, hellgrammites, or almost any baitfish on or near the bottom could produce a nice bass. Smallmouth bass don't grow as big as largemouth bass and are found in slightly different habitats. Smallmouth bass prefer cool to cold water, while largemouth bass prefer warm water. Most smallmouth bass range in size from 1 to 3 pounds, but a 5-pound smallmouth is not uncommon. Remember, when using live baits such as crayfish and shiners, let the fish run a bit before hooking it. The rule my father taught me was to let the fish run until it stops, wait a minute, and then hook it.

Yellow Perch

PERCA FLAVESCENS

8–12 inches

Yellow perch are good-looking fish. They are golden-yellow with six or more dark, vertical bands on their sides. The most striking feature is their orange-red pelvic, pectoral, and anal fins. They can grow to about 16 inches but average much smaller. Although yellow perch have a similar body structure to a few related fish, such as walleye and the darters, they are distinctive enough and common enough that fishermen don't confuse them with these other species. Yellow perch have two separated dorsal fins, like walleye and darters, an otherwise uncommon feature in northeastern freshwater fish. The anterior dorsal fin is spiny and the posterior dorsal fin is soft and fleshy.

Yellow perch are very common in almost every freshwater lake, pond, and slow-moving river and stream throughout the Northeast and much of the rest of the United States. They spawn in the spring, in the shallows and among the vegetation. Yellow perch spawn a bit earlier than sunfish and other warm-water species. In the summer months, they tend to school up and go into deeper water where it is cooler. In the fall, they come back into the shallows to feed.

Many people consider yellow perch to be the best-eating species of panfish. Charter boats go out on Lake Erie and other large lakes strictly for the purpose of catching yellow perch, although most fishermen simply encounter them while fishing for other species that populate the same habitat. They are easy and fun to catch with flies, spinners, spoon lures, and most any small live bait such as worms and small shiners. They go after your bait aggressively and put up a good fight. Yellow perch are active all year and can be taken readily through the ice in the winter. Small jigs and small shiners are the preferred baits for ice fishing. They are great fish for children to catch, but beware of the spiny dorsal fin when removing the hook.

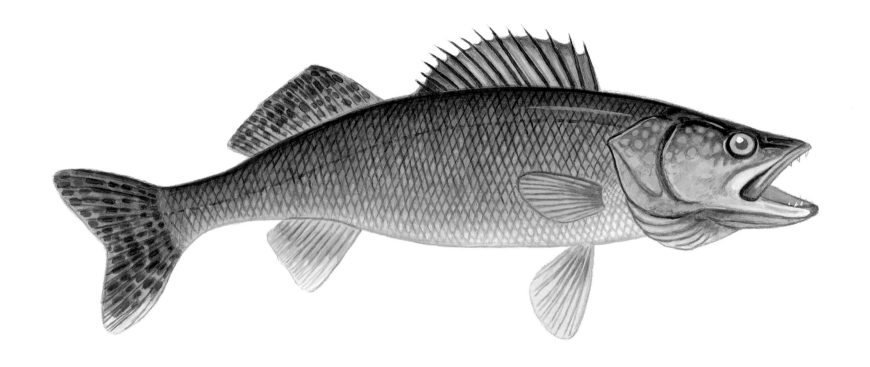

Walleye

SANDER VITREUS

18–25 inches

Walleye are in the perch family and most closely resemble yellow perch in shape, but not in color or markings. They most often are olive-brown to almost yellowish overall, occasionally with irregular bronze markings lightly scattered on the sides. They generally are much larger than yellow perch. They can grow to over 20 inches and occasionally reach 10 pounds or more. However, they average about 1 to 2 pounds.

Walleye have streamlined bodies and large mouths with big canine teeth. Their double dorsal fin is separated into a spiny anterior and a fleshy posterior fin. Two characteristics distinguish walleye from other similar species: They have a dark blotch or segment on the posterior base of their front dorsal fin, and a white section in the lower tip of their caudal fin.

Walleye are named for their large, somewhat milky-looking eyes. Their eyes are very sensitive to light and they tend to avoid it, yet they actually have better vision than other fish in low-light conditions. They tend to be dusk-to-dawn feeders, rather than daytime feeders, although they may venture out to feed in the daytime if they inhabit murky water or if there is a thick overcast. Otherwise, they spend the daytime hours hiding under overhangs and large debris in the water. Walleye do best in very large lakes and rivers that are turbid and murky, and rarely are found in shallow lakes and rivers with very clear water, or in small ponds and streams. They like moderately cool, rather deep water, but often come into more shallow water at night to feed. They also go into the shallows for a short time to spawn in the early spring. Spawning most often takes place at night. Walleye are often found in schools.

Walleye are native to middle North America from the Rockies to the Appalachian Mountains, but have been introduced to many areas in the Northeast. They are the most popular gamefish in many locations because of their large size and ability to put up a wild fight, not to mention their tender and tasty fillets. Their diet mostly consists of smaller fish, but they are known to feed on crayfish, leeches, insects, insect larvae, and other aquatic animals. Fishing techniques for catching large walleye vary from location to location, but commonly include the use of such live baits as night crawlers, crayfish, and shiners, or artificial baits including crank baits, jigs, spinners, and spoons.

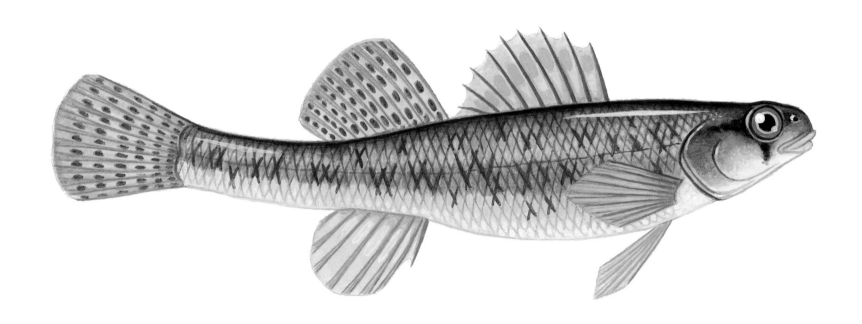

Johnny Darter

ETHEOSTOMA NIGRUM

Approximately 3.5 inches

We have included some common fish that can be captured only with a net, yet are quite interesting and unique. Johnny darters are obscure because they grow only to 3.5 inches and would not be caught on a fishing line. Despite being unknown to most anglers, johnny darters actually are quite common around the Northeast and much of the rest of the United States. A few other darters are found in the Northeast, but johnny darters are the most common. They most closely resemble swamp darters. Johnny darters have a double dorsal fin separated into an anterior spiny portion and a posterior fleshy portion. They are sandy to grayish overall, with scattered brown specks. Distinctive W- or X-shaped markings on their sides distinguish johnny darters from other darters.

I often netted these fish for my biology classroom aquarium to demonstrate a characteristic of johnny darters and other darters: They have no air bladders. Without these bladders, which allow fish to maintain the same density as the water, johnny darters are always denser than the water. They "dart" when they swim and then sink to the bottom, where they spend most of their lives. They feed on small crustaceans, insect larvae, and other small animals in the streams, ponds, and rivers they inhabit.

Most freshwater fish possess an air bladder (also known as a gas bladder or swim bladder). It is made up of two flexible sacs in the dorsal part of the body cavity. Simply put, its function is to make adjustments in a fish's density, allowing the fish to maintain neutral buoyancy as it ascends or descends in the water. In this way, a fish does not have to expend extra energy struggling to hold its position near the surface, along the bottom, or somewhere in between. Gas is typically added to or removed from the air bladder through the bloodstream, although some fish can gulp air. In a few species, the air bladder also can function as a respiratory organ (like a lung) or a sound resonator.

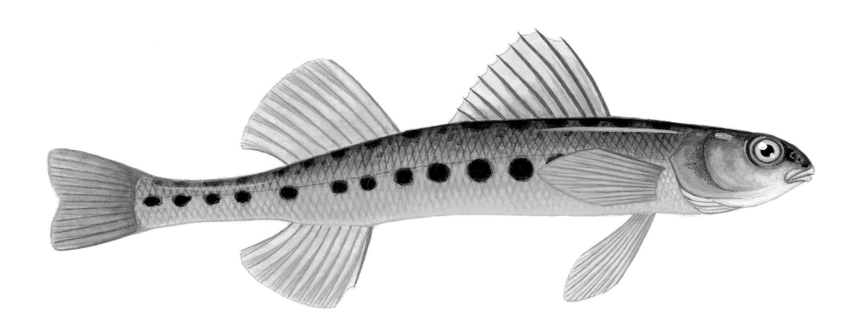

Eastern Sand Darter

AMMOCRYPTA PELLUCIDA

Approximately 2.5 inches

Eastern sand darters have elongated, slender bodies, with a series of large, dark dots along the sides and the dorsal midline. They are light yellow with an almost translucent appearance. They have two widely separated dorsal fins, a spiny anterior fin and a fleshy posterior fin. They have no scales on their ventral surface.

With no air bladder, like other darters, eastern sand darters tend to spend much of their time on the sandy bottom of streams and rivers. They often burrow into the soft, sandy bottom and bury themselves, with only their eyes protruding. This may be to conserve energy or to hide from predators, or may allow them to attack prey more effectively. They feed mostly on small insect larvae and small crustaceans.

Eastern sand darters are found as far west as the Mississippi drainage and north to the Great Lakes region into New York, Vermont, and a scattering of other places in the Northeast toward the Canadian border. They inhabit mostly moderate-sized streams and small rivers with a fine sandy bottom. A general rule is that the current has to be strong enough to prevent the deposit of large amounts of silt but slow enough that the fine sandy bottom is not washed away. They also inhabit some sandy-bottomed lakes and ponds, including Lake Erie in New York.

Eastern sand darters might have been much more widespread in the past. Their decline may be due to their very specific habitat requirements. The use of land around rivers and streams for agricultural purposes often causes the deposit of higher than normal amounts of silt on the bottom and the general loss of water quality. Dams built along rivers separate populations of the species and affect their continued existence in some areas.

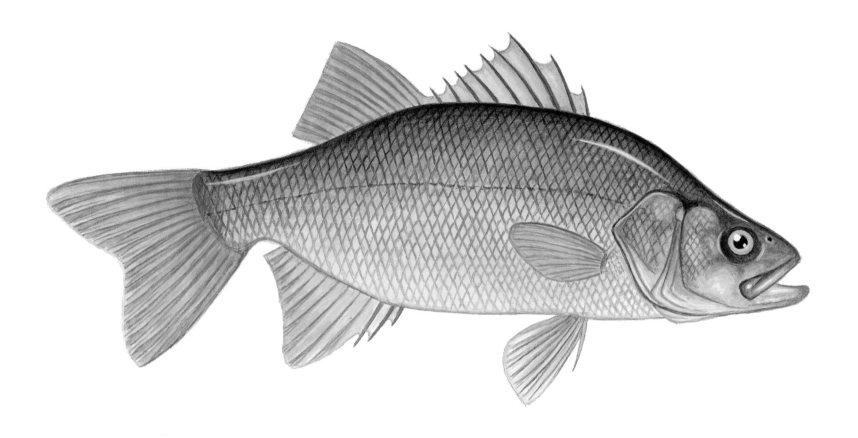

White Perch

MORONE AMERICANUS

7–12 inches

Despite their name, white perch are a relative of striped and white bass. They are smaller and stouter than striped bass, but look fairly similar to white bass. Fishermen sometimes confuse them with largemouth bass. However, they do not have the dark lateral bands found on largemouth bass and they have much smaller mouths. Other than their lateral lines, white perch have no lines or stripes on their body. They usually have a dark greenish gray back, quickly tapering into silvery green to white on their sides and belly. They may appear iridescent in the right light. Their body is deepest at the point just before the anterior dorsal fin. This arch is most dramatic in older, larger members.

White perch are semi-anadromous fish, living most of their lives in estuarine waters, but spawning in freshwater. Their native range is the brackish waters and estuaries of the Atlantic coast from Nova Scotia to South Carolina, from which they move well inland up freshwater rivers and streams to spawn. Their range has been expanded into lakes and reservoirs beyond their native habitats by various intentional and accidental stockings over the years. In these situations, they are landlocked and remain in freshwater throughout their lives. White perch have made their way into the Great Lakes and the Mississippi drainage through the system of canals that connect the Saint Lawrence River to these other bodies of water for shipping purposes.

Despite their popularity as a very tasty panfish, white perch have been blamed in numerous bodies of water beyond their native habitats for reducing the populations of such native fish as walleye and white bass by eating their eggs during spring spawning.

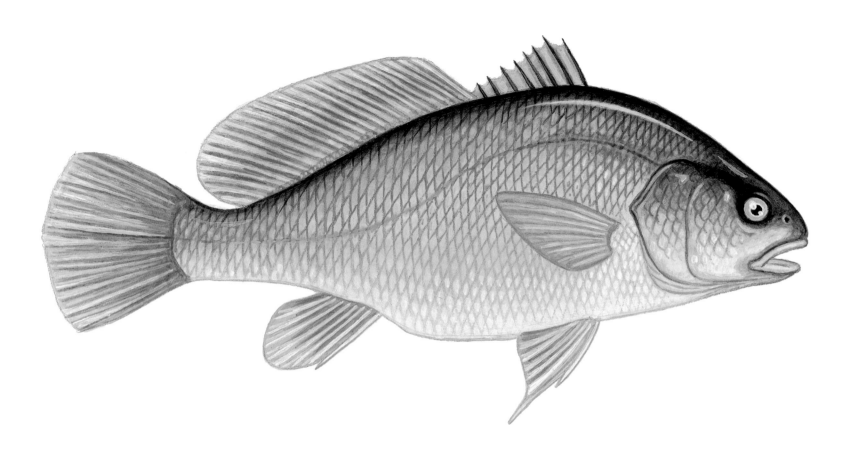

Freshwater Drum

APLODINOTUS GRUNNIENS

Approximately 15 inches

Freshwater drum are a very wide fish, with a bit of a hump behind a large, broad head. They have large, slightly turned-down mouths. They usually are silvery grey, on the sides and toward the dorsal surface, sometimes with a tinge of purple, and white toward the belly. Their large scales are very shiny. They have a double dorsal fin. The anterior part is spiny and barely connected to the posterior dorsal fin, which is long and fleshy. They also have a lateral line that travels right through the caudal fin.

Their name comes from the fact that males make a drumming and croaking noise with specialized muscles that vibrate against the air bladder, causing it to vibrate. These noises probably have something to do with spawning. Native Americans called them buffalo fish because the noise reminded them of the grunts that buffalo make.

Freshwater drum have the largest north-to-south range of any freshwater fish in North America. They are found from the Hudson Bay area of Canada to Guatemala in Central America and from the east side of the Rocky Mountains to the west side of the Appalachians. They are found most commonly in large rivers and lakes. In the Northeast, their range is limited to the Saint Lawrence River drainage, some of the bigger lakes in New York State, and Lake Champlain in Vermont.

They are the only freshwater members of the drum family. They favor clean, clear water with gravel bottom, but will tolerate turbid water and muddy bottoms. The freshwater drum is a nocturnal feeder, foraging for insect larvae, snails, clams, and minnows near or on the bottom.

Freshwater drum are not widely sought after by anglers as a gamefish.

Baitfishing on the bottom at night is the best time to catch one, although you can catch them during the day. They put up a surprisingly good fight and grow quite large. Over 5 pounds is not common, but they have been known to grow to well over 20 pounds and the world record is 54.5 pounds. Drum have a long life span, with some known to have lived well over twenty years.

There is a wide disagreement on whether they are a good fish to eat. They are caught commercially in the Mississippi River and some of the Great Lakes, and sold widely. Their fillets are not considered high quality but some find them delicious. If you catch one, you will just have to try it for yourself and form your own opinion.

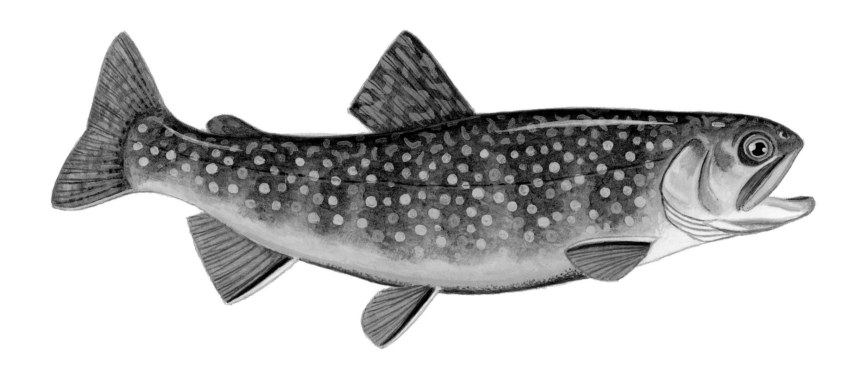

Brook Trout

SALVELINUS FONTINALIS

8–12 inches

Some people might confuse brook trout with other common trout of New England, such as rainbow or brown trout, because the general body shapes and structures are all very similar, and because all trout species have a small adipose fin on the upper surface of the body between the dorsal fin and the caudal fin. However, brook trout are olive-green, with red spots highlighted in blue and light yellow to gold spots on the dorsal half of the body. Their pectoral, pelvic, and anal fins all have a white anterior edge, followed by a thin strip of black, with the rest of the fin being orange in color.

Brook trout are found naturally in the cold, clean water of small streams, ponds, and rivers, where they feed mostly on aquatic insect larvae and nymphs, as well as terrestrial insects. They are stocked widely around the Northeast, but are also native to many locations. Native brook trout tend to be smaller than hatchery-grown individuals. Brook trout are the most common trout in the Northeast. They are the state fish of New Hampshire, Vermont, New York, Pennsylvania, and New Jersey.

They are the perfect fish to get kids interested in fishing. They are relatively easy to catch with light tackle, just using worms and walking along a small brook or river. They can also be caught on a variety of artificial flies and lures. They are aggressive fighters and don't have to be very big to be enjoyable gamefish. They are very edible and easy to clean, so children may learn how to clean them easily.

One of my favorite flies for brook trout was the Bruno Streamer. You probably haven't heard of it, because Bruno was my childhood dog; the streamer was made out of his long, fluffy, white fur. We used to make a variety of other streamers, but it always seemed we caught most of our trout on Bruno's fur. When he died, I cut off a piece of his fur before we buried him. Initially, I felt bad that I had done that, but later I felt even worse, when I ran out of fur for Bruno Streamers.

Brown Trout

SALMO TRUTTA

10–16 inches

Brown trout have a dark dorsal surface and are generally a shiny, light brownish color on their sides. Black spots dominate the upper sides of the body, with red spots in the middle, each surrounded by bluish or silver halos. Their fins and body shape are typical for a trout, with a single, soft dorsal fin and an adipose fin located back toward the tail. The caudal fin is almost square. Their coloration and markings are rather distinctive, making them easy to distinguish from other trout. However, they are sometimes confused with Atlantic salmon when their coloration is less brown and more silvery than usual.

Brown trout first were introduced into the United States from their native Europe in the 1880s. They now are stocked widely in the Northeast and have done well enough to produce some natural populations where the conditions and habitat are well suited for spawning. They can withstand higher water temperatures and lower oxygen levels than other trout, making them a hardy fish to stock.

Brown trout can be cautious and somewhat difficult to catch. They feed on insects, particularly larvae and nymphs. They also feed on crayfish, snails, small frogs, and other fish. My father often would catch brown trout on hellgrammites—the larval stage of a dobsonfly—when no one else seemed to be able to catch anything. Dawn or dusk seem to be the best times for catching browns. They can be among the largest gamefish in the Northeast, with an occasional fish coming in at 10 pounds or more. The big ones usually are taken in lakes or large ponds. A population of smelt or other forage fish tends to help produce the large ones. Trolling with spoons or spinners or using live bait such as shiners or smelt might be effective. And don't forget the hellgrammites!

Hellgrammites are rather intimidating little critters. They have large mandibles in the front that can bite you, and a hard palate on the thorax behind their head. They tend to last a long time and stay on the hook when hooked through the hard palate. If left on the bottom too long, they will crawl under rocks and logs, and get your line stuck, so it is best to move them from time to time. To catch hellgrammites, stand in fast, shallow water in any rocky stream or river. Simply kick around the rocks while holding a dip net downstream and the hellgrammites will drift into the net. You can gather quite a few in a short amount of time any time of the year. Most fishermen have never used them, yet they are a natural bait for trout and bass.

Rainbow Trout

ONCORHYNCHUS MYKISS

8–16 inches

Rainbow trout have the same shape and fin placement as other common trout, but they are generally silvery in color and generously covered in small, black spots throughout their body and fins, except on the lower sides and belly. The spots are more concentrated toward the dorsal surface. Their name comes from the bright pink to red band that runs along each side from the operculum to the tail, making rainbow trout a colorful and beautiful fish.

Rainbow trout are native to the western United States, but have been introduced into the Northeast and around the world by widespread stocking. Rainbows aren't as successful as brook and brown trout in reproducing naturally in their introduced habitats, and spawning in the Northeast is quite rare. Rainbow populations outside their native range are almost totally dependent on stockings of captive-bred fish.

As a gamefish, they may be among the best fighters, attacking lures and natural baits with great intensity. Live bait, such as shiners, worms, or salmon eggs, will catch rainbows. They are particularly fun to catch fly-fishing using streamers and other wet or dry flies. They often will jump clear out of the water as you reel them in. Rainbows tend to average about 1 to 2 pounds in weight, but under the right conditions, they may exceed 7 or 8 pounds.

Rainbow trout and steelhead trout are actually the same species. The name "steelhead" refers to the anadromous version that lives in the ocean and migrates up rivers to spawn. This happens most often on the West Coast in the Pacific Ocean. Some sea-run steelhead trout are found along the Northeast coast, but they are not very common. "Steelhead" also can refer to rainbow trout that are found in the Great Lakes, including Lake Erie in New York, which sometimes spawn up rivers and tributaries leading into the lakes.

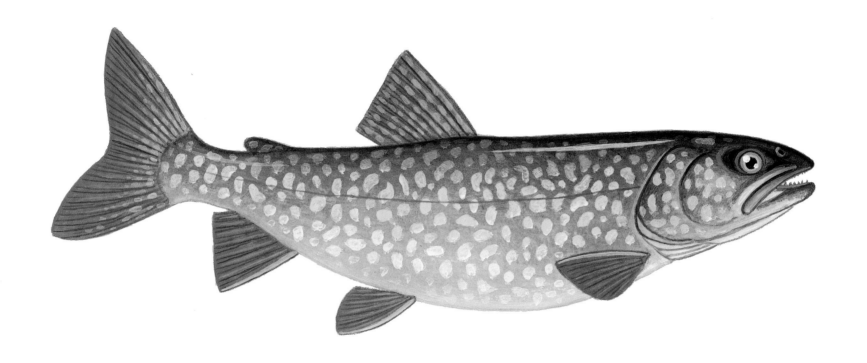

Lake Trout

SALVELINUS NAMAYCUSH

18–24 inches

L ake trout have the typical trout body structure. They are not as colorful as many of the other trout species, but are still nice-looking. They are dark grayish blue on the dorsal surface, and light silvery gray on the sides. They become lighter toward the belly, which is white. Irregularly shaped pale spots cover the body and fins. The caudal fin is deeply forked.

Lake trout inhabit very deep lakes and ponds. In the spring, when surface water is still cold enough, they may feed near the surface and in the shallows, where food is more plentiful. They feed on aquatic larvae and nymphs, and crayfish, but mostly on small fish. Early spring is a great time to fish for lake trout, because they are feeding more actively on a variety of food. Trolling near the surface with lures, flies, or live baitfish such as smelt can be very effective, especially just after ice-out. Downriggers are needed in the summer months when the fish are very deep. You can also fish with worms, salmon eggs, or shiners in the deep water in the summer. In the winter, lake trout can be taken through the ice using tip-ups with live baitfish. Jigging with shiny spoon lures or jigs, with a smelt or piece of bait attached, is very popular in some locations.

I have heard people complain that lake trout don't put up a very good fight when you catch them. This is likely because most anglers hook their lake trout in the late spring and summer in very deep water. Normally, fish swim from deep to shallower water quite slowly, allowing their air bladder to make the adjustment. When you rapidly reel any fish to the surface from depths of 60 feet or more, its air bladder expands rapidly because it cannot send the air back into the bloodstream fast enough. This expansion of the bladder exerts pressure on the organs and the blood vessels in the abdominal cavity, inhibiting a lake trout from putting up a good battle. Catching a nice laker in shallower water in the early spring could be a more exciting encounter.

Blueback Trout

SALVELINUS ALPINUS OQUASSA

8–15 inches

Blueback trout have a dark, bluish black dorsal surface, becoming silvery gray on the sides and white on the belly. They have light spots, similar to brook trout, and are sometimes confused with them. Their tails have a forked caudal fin that is different than brook trout, which have nearly square tails. Their pectoral and pelvic fins are often bright orange to red on the outer margins with a white and a black rim on the anterior end, somewhat like a brook trout. During spawning season, in the late fall into early winter, they become much more colorful, with orange to pinkish bellies and much brighter color in the fins. The spots on their sides become more colorful as well.

Blueback trout or landlocked Arctic char are found in high-latitude freshwater lakes around the globe. They have the most northerly distribution of any trout. The only native populations in the United States are in Alaska and Maine. An anadromous (sea-run) version of this species spawns up freshwater northern rivers around the globe. There is much confusion among taxonomists concerning the landlocked version of this species of trout and its link to the Sunapee trout. They share the same genus and species, but most agree that they are somewhat different, leading to a variety of common and Latin names.

Bluebacks are an elusive trout that spend the summer months in the very deep, cold-water lakes of northern Maine and parts of Canada. They are native in about twelve lakes in the northern half of Maine. They have been introduced in other lakes, but they do not do well where lake trout and Atlantic salmon have been introduced. They were once a very abundant trout in the Rangeley Lakes in Maine and were served in all the inns and hotel restaurants in the area in the late 1800s. However, when smelt and landlocked Atlantic salmon were introduced into the Rangeley Lakes, the smelt competed for food and the salmon preyed on the blueback trout. In a very short time, they were exterminated from the Rangeley Lakes. Similar situations happened in New Hampshire and Vermont and now the blueback trout is found only in a limited number of lakes in Maine. Efforts are underway to protect blueback trout in Maine by controlling or eliminating stocking of other trout and salmon species into the lakes where the blueback is considered a native species. Also, controls on the use of certain baitfish are being considered.

Fishing for bluebacks is a challenge. In the summer, they are found in the coldest, most oxygenated water—usually the deepest part of the lake. To catch one, you have to troll very deep with downriggers or use jigs or live bait. In the spring and fall, they may remain in shallow water after spawning, and fly-fishing using a Grey Ghost or a Black Ghost might produce a fish. Trolling in rather shallow water with lures may be successful as well. Some people spend a lifetime trying to catch just one. An eleven-year-old boy set the Maine record for blueback trout in August of 2008 with a 5.24-pound, 25.4-inch-long fish. The previous record of 4 pounds, 4 ounces had been held for thirty-five years.

Atlantic Salmon

SALMO SALAR

Approximately 18 inches

Atlantic salmon have a trout-like shape, with a forked caudal fin and an adipose fin on the dorsal surface. The sides are silvery, with scattered dark specks or X-shaped markings. The dorsal surface is a darker bluish gray to olive-brown with a silvery look. The belly is silvery white. Spawning adults can develop red to orange splotches or highlights on their sides. Males develop an elongated head or snout and a hooked lower jaw before spawning.

Atlantic salmon are anadromous. They are native to the northeastern coast of North America, Greenland, Iceland, and northwestern Europe and Asia. In the northeastern United States, Atlantic salmon are king of the gamefish. They not only spawn up many rivers from the Connecticut River to Newfoundland and Labrador, but they have become landlocked in almost every major lake and some rivers in New England and New York. Some lakes have self-sustaining populations, while others need the support of hatchery-grown fish, because an insufficient number of rivers or streams enter the lake for the salmon to migrate up to spawn. Some limited spawning occurs in these lakes, but they can't produce enough offspring to repopulate the lake each year.

Atlantic salmon make their way up rivers and streams along the northeastern coast of North America in the fall to spawn. Females dig out nests in gravel- or sandy-bottomed streams in preparation for spawning. Young fish may remain in their freshwater birthplace for one to six years before making their way to the ocean, where they spend a few more years growing to maturity before returning to the same river where they were hatched. Landlocked individuals spawn in much the same way, migrating up streams and rivers that enter their natal lakes. Young landlocked Atlantic salmon spend one or two years in the river where they were hatched before traveling down to the lake, and return to the same river or stream to spawn a few years later. Females take a little longer than males to mature and return. Unlike Pacific salmon, Atlantic salmon do not die after spawning and may return to their spawning grounds for several years.

They feed on almost any invertebrates in the water, including surface insects, insect larvae and nymphs, and crayfish. However, other fish comprise the most important part of their diet. The introduction of smelt and alewife into large lakes as forage has added to the success of landlocked Atlantic salmon as a species and gamefish.

Atlantic salmon are highly esteemed as food and as a gamefish, and are considered even more special because they are native to the Northeast. They are powerful fighters, digging deep into the river or lake once hooked, while others jump clear out of the water again and again as you reel them in. Landlocked salmon average about 18 inches in length and weigh 2 or 3 pounds, and sometimes can be much larger.

Coho Salmon

ONCORHYNCHUS KISUTCH

Approximately 24 inches (2 feet)

Coho salmon are bluish gray on the head and back, changing quickly to shiny silver on the sides, and white on the belly. They have small black spots on their body and caudal fin, mostly above the lateral line. Spawning adults become deep red, almost maroon, on their sides and bellies. Males develop a slight arch in their back and a slight hook in their jaw.

Coho salmon are anadromous fish that normally live in the ocean, spawning up rivers and large streams along the northwestern coast of the United States and Canada, and into Alaska. They are also found along the Asian coast of the Pacific Ocean from northern Japan and northward along the Russian coast. They have been introduced into many lakes around the United States, including all of the Great Lakes.

Totally self-sustaining populations of coho salmon are not common in freshwater lakes, because not enough suitable rivers and streams exist to produce a sufficient number of offspring. Hatchery stockings supplement most freshwater populations. However, some natural reproduction takes place in the Great Lakes and other large lakes where these salmon have been introduced. Lake coho salmon spawn from September through October by swimming up rivers and streams that enter the lake. Females dig out nests of rocks and gravel and lay two to five thousand eggs. The males fertilize the eggs as they pass over the nesting area. Adult coho salmon die soon after spawning, as do most Pacific salmon. The young may spend a year or more in the stream where they are hatched, and return to the same location in three to five years to spawn on their own.

Adult landlocked coho salmon feed largely on other fish, but insects make up a fair amount of their diet in the spring. The average lake coho salmon weighs 5 to 8 pounds and is about 24 inches in length. Spring is the best time to fish for landlocked coho salmon, when they congregate in the shallower waters near the shore. Casting or trolling with colorful lures, spinners, streamers, and other flies is popular among anglers, and night crawlers, minnows, or cut bait are smart choices for catching these salmon. They are a popular gamefish because of their large size, fierce fighting, and jumping abilities. They are excellent eating fish.

Kokanee Salmon / Breeding Kokanee Salmon

ONCORHYNCHUS NERKA

Approximately 10 inches

Kokanee salmon have a bluish green dorsal surface, silvery sides, and a white belly. Unlike most salmon and trout, kokanee have no spots on their sides or caudal fin. During spawning season, both males and females turn dark red with greenish heads. Males also develop a humped back and a hook in their jaw. They are quite small as salmon go, reaching a maximum length of 15 or 16 inches, but averaging only about 10 inches, much smaller than the ocean-dwelling sockeye salmon.

Kokanee have a very unusual diet for a salmon. They mostly feed on plankton, using their modified gill rakers to strain out the minute organisms as they swim. If the water stays cool enough, they tend to spend much of their time near the surface. In the summer months, they sometimes go deeper where the water is cooler. Occasionally, they feed on other small invertebrates and very tiny fish.

Kokanee salmon are the landlocked version of the anadromous sockeye salmon. Despite some minor variations in characteristics, they share the same genus and species name. They are native to the northwestern United States, British Columbia, Canada, and most of Alaska. They have been introduced into large lakes in several states, including a few in the Northeast. The largest introduced populations in the Northeast have been in New York and a few lakes in Connecticut. Attempts to introduce them into other lakes have taken place in Massachusetts and Maine with varying amounts of success. These introductions don't always succeed because they don't have suitable places to spawn.

Kokanee salmon spawn between August and November by swimming up available rivers or streams that spill into the lakes they inhabit. They don't travel as far as the ocean-dwelling members do. When rivers or streams are not available, kokanee will spawn along the gravelly shore of the lake. Females dig out a patch of gravel and rocks, where they spawn up to two thousand eggs.

Kokanee are a delicious salmon to eat. Many prize their pink meat. They are best eaten before they start traveling upriver to spawn, because they become a bit mushy and less tasty at that time. Because they feed mostly on plankton, they are not easy to catch with a hook and line, although they may take small baits such as salmon eggs or worms, or small lures. They probably attack lures for territorial reasons rather than for food. Kokanee have small, delicate mouths, so take your time reeling them in.

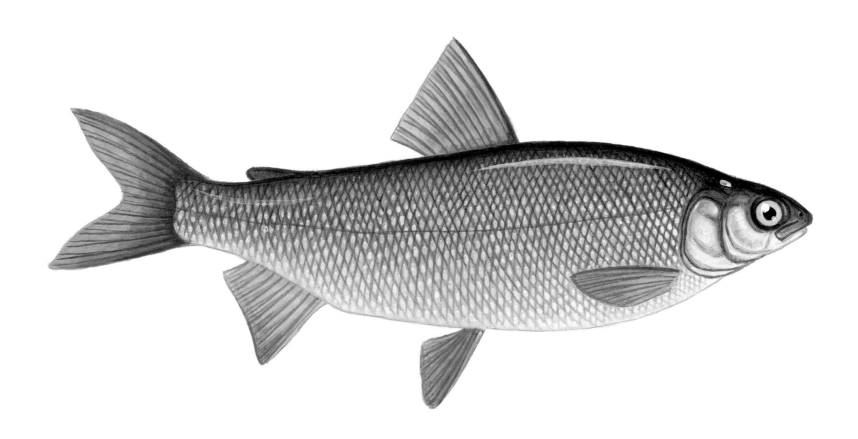

Lake Whitefish

COREGONUS CLUPEAFORMIS

15–20 inches

Lake whitefish are members of the trout/salmon family. They have a rather stout body, blunt head, and small, delicate mouth with no teeth. They have the adipose dorsal fin and general body shape of salmon and trout. The biggest differences are their smaller mouths and larger, visible scales. The caudal fin is deeply forked and their fins are very light in color except for some black streaks and highlights. Their dorsal surface is olive-green to bluish gray, with silvery white sides and belly. They are similar in appearance to round whitefish, except that round whitefish have a more rounded body and orange fins.

Lake whitefish are native to many of the locations they inhabit, including many lakes in the Northeast, where they spend most of their time in very deep, cool water, sometimes at 100 to 200 feet or even deeper. They are generally bottom feeders, with a diet of small invertebrates such as insect larvae, small crustaceans, and small mollusks that live in the gravel and rocks on the bottom. They will also feed on very small fish and the eggs of other fish. Lake whitefish are a schooling fish and often spend their time with other members of their species. They live a long time and may weigh 1 to 4 pounds.

Lake whitefish are a popular commercially fished species in the Great Lakes, and are among the best eating freshwater fish in North America. Millions of pounds are taken each year in Canada and the United States. However, the amount taken now is not nearly as much as it once was.

In the Northeast, they are found in most of the large lakes throughout New England and New York. They have become more popular as a gamefish in recent years, perhaps because anglers are becoming more educated about their habits and how to catch them, and are attracted by the challenge of nabbing a difficult and elusive fish. Their feeding habits and tendency to spend most of their lives in deep water make them a formidable challenge.

Most lake whitefish in the Northeast are caught in the winter through the ice in moderately deep water, using small baits such as cut-up baitfish, salmon eggs, or even worms. Many ice fishermen use baited jigs and spoons, bouncing them on the bottom. The same baits can be used in the summer, but the water must be 100 feet deep or more. Lake whitefish do not strike fiercely at the bait, and they are difficult to feel at first in deep water, unless you fish directly over them to feel their tug. In the fall and into the winter, they can be found in shallower water as they prepare to spawn. This is often a good time to catch them if the fishing season is still open where you are fishing. In the spring, they often go to where other fish are spawning and feed on their eggs. During this time, they can be taken on flies and salmon eggs. Using a single egg on a small hook to accommodate their small mouths seems to be good method.

Round Whitefish

PROSOPIUM CYLINDRACEUM

10–15 inches

Round whitefish have the same general body shape and characteristics as salmon and trout, with a more rounded and cylindrical body. This roundness in their midsection gives them their name. The dorsal surface most often is olive-brown, quickly changing to silver on the sides and silvery white on the belly. The fins, particularly the pelvic, pectoral, and anal fins, are light orange. The mouth is smaller than that of most trout and salmon and round whitefish are toothless as adults. The upper jaw extends slightly beyond the lower jaw. The scales are quite large and visible, unlike those of most trout and salmon. Round whitefish have the typical salmonid adipose fin between the dorsal and caudal fins, and a deeply forked caudal fin, similar to an Atlantic salmon. They tend to be slow growers and average about 10 to 15 inches in length, though it was common in the past to catch individuals 18 inches or even longer.

Round whitefish are bottom feeders and spend most of their time in deep water foraging in the rocks and gravel for tiny snails and clams, insect larvae and nymphs, crustaceans, small fish, and sometimes the eggs of other fish such as lake trout.

Round whitefish were once more abundant throughout the cold-water lakes and a few rivers in the Northeast, but they recently have become scarce in many areas. The sometimes over-populated yellow perch is blamed for feeding on their eggs and juveniles, and the stocking of certain species of salmon may have helped diminish their numbers. Salmon are known to feed on the round whitefish's young.

Round whitefish are not caught frequently because they spend most of their time in 120 to 150 feet of water and usually don't feed on typical baits used to catch lake trout and other deep-water species. They occasionally are taken through the ice in the winter using smaller baits such as worms, salmon eggs, or small baitfish. The round whitefish is protected in New York State by the Endangered Species Act and you are not allowed to fish for them. If you accidentally catch one, you must release it immediately.

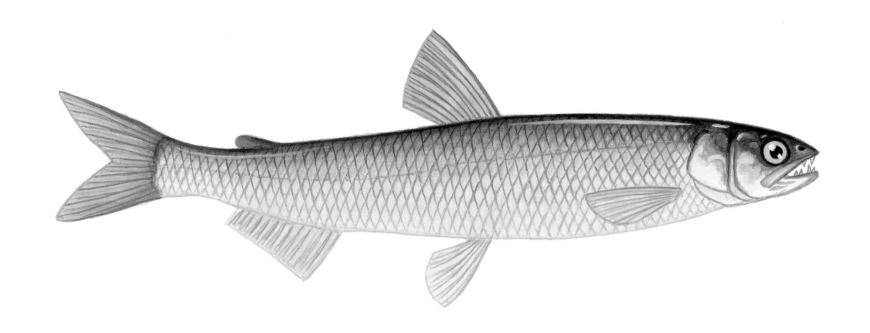

American Smelt

OSMERUS MORDAX

Approximately 6 inches

American smelt are long, slender, silvery-colored fish with a general appearance and shape that is somewhat similar to a trout. Their dorsal surface is greenish, and some individuals have a pink to purplish blue gleam that lends them their other common name, rainbow smelt. They have a small adipose dorsal fin like trout and catfish. The caudal fin is deeply forked and they have visible scales.

American smelt are anadromous fish that live along the Atlantic coast from Labrador to New Jersey. Each spring, they migrate up rivers and streams to spawn. They also have been introduced into many large lakes, ponds, and reservoirs in the Northeast and have become landlocked. They inhabit all of the Great Lakes. American smelt have become an important forage species for large trout and salmon throughout the Northeast and elsewhere. In freshwater lakes, smelt tend to favor deeper water and they most often are seen traveling in schools. They feed on small insect larvae and nymphs, and other small fish.

Although they are considered a small fish, smelt can grow up to 9 inches. Despite this small size, they are considered very good eating. They are sought after for food but also are used as baitfish to catch trout and salmon. Along the coast, smelt are netted in the spring as they head upstream to spawn. They usually are frozen quickly and sent to restaurants and stores throughout the United States. The landlocked members are also caught as they spawn up rivers and streams from the lakes they inhabit. However, rules on fishing for smelt vary from state to state.

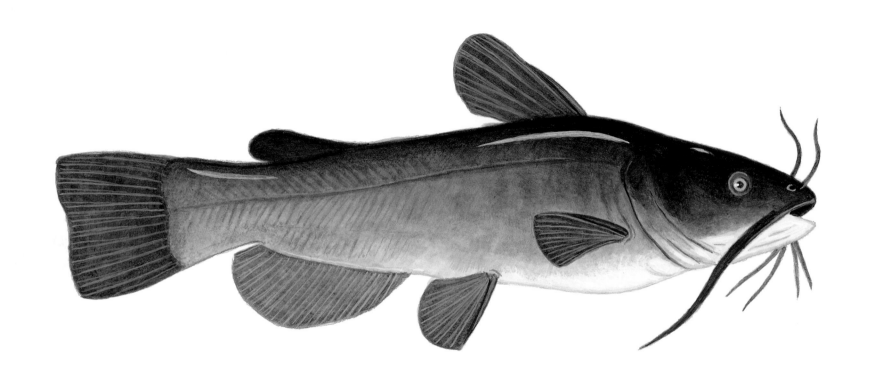

Brown Bullhead

ICTALURUS NEBULOSUS

6–10 inches

Brown bullheads are very common in the Northeast. They are a variety of catfish, with eight barbels around their mouth and no scales. They range from olive-brown to almost black, with a yellowish to white belly. Their sides sometimes can be a bit blotchy and mottled. Their scaleless skin is very smooth and slimy. They have a small dorsal fin and an adipose fin on their dorsal surface. The caudal fin is almost square, sometimes with a slight indentation. The body is rather thick, with a flattened head and a wide mouth. They look most like yellow bullheads. However, brown bullheads have dark chin barbels and yellow bullheads have whitish chin barbels.

Brown bullheads are common from Maine to Florida and west to Texas, Missouri, and into Canada. They are found in most warm-water lakes, ponds, and slow-moving streams and rivers. They are nocturnal bottom feeders, consuming a wide variety of food, including small mollusks, crayfish, insects, insect larvae and nymphs, small fish, and even algae and other plant matter. Although they may prefer clean water, they can tolerate warmer water temperatures, lower oxygen levels, and higher levels of water pollution than many other fish. They are a very hardy fish. They can even survive for hours out of the water if kept cool and moist.

The best time to catch brown bullheads is toward dusk and into the night. They feed by smell and use their barbels to help detect food. You can catch them on almost any live bait, but a worm sitting on the bottom works as well as anything. They can grow to more than 15 inches, but most brown bullheads are 6 to 10 inches long. They have a sharp, bony spine in the dorsal fin and two pectoral fins. These spines are very rigid, so beware when removing your hook to avoid a painful puncture in your hand or finger. Like other members of the catfish family, brown bullheads are sought after for their tasty meat. They can be difficult to clean, but if you catch enough of them, they make a delicious meal.

Yellow Bullhead

ICTALURUS NATALIS

8–10 inches

Yellow bullheads most closely resemble brown bullheads. However, their heads are less flattened and more blocky and blunt than those of brown bullheads, and the four barbels on the lower jaw are white rather than black. Yellow bullheads have a distinguishing light band passing horizontally through the anal fin, and generally are lighter olive-brown with highlights of yellow showing through. They sometimes have slight mottling on their sides. Their light bellies are usually white to yellow. The caudal fin is slightly rounded and not quite square like that of the brown bullhead.

Yellow bullheads are most common in the eastern and southern United States and west to the Mississippi River drainage. In the Northeast, they are not as common as brown bullheads and were introduced in some of the areas where they now exist. They prefer weedy, shallow ponds and slow-moving streams and rivers. They like cool, clean water, but will tolerate warmer water. They don't do very well where the water is murky and filled with silt, and are not as tolerant of polluted waters as brown bullheads. They spawn under embankments in streams and rivers and use vegetation, stumps, and logs as cover for their eggs in ponds and lakes. They spawn a bit earlier than brown bullheads.

Yellow bullheads are easy to catch with worms and other live bait. They feed by smell, mostly at night. However, they sometimes will bite during the daytime, particularly when it is overcast. They are a very exciting fish for kids to catch because of their odd looks and "cat whiskers." Like other catfish, the meat of the yellow bullhead is flavorful. They are not a fish that anglers tend to seek out, but if you know a location where you could catch a bunch of them, they would make a great meal. Like brown bullheads, yellow bullheads have sharp spines in their dorsal and pectoral fins, so take care when catching and handling them.

Channel Catfish

ICTALURUS PUNCTATUS

12–24 inches (1–2 feet)

Channel catfish are the largest catfish in the Northeast and should not be confused with any other catfish, with their long, tapered bodies, pointed head, and deeply forked caudal fin. They are rather dark olive-brown on the dorsal surface to lighter olive-brown on the sides, with irregularly shaped dark specks that become less obvious as they get older. Their bellies most often are white. They have four dark barbels on the upper jaw and four slightly lighter barbels on the lower jaw.

Channel catfish are native to most of the large river drainages of the central United States. When you think of channel catfish, you probably think of the Mississippi and other large rivers in that area. They are not common in the Northeast, but they do exist in many large rivers and lakes, including the Connecticut River, Saint Lawrence River, Lake Erie and the other Great Lakes, Lake Champlain, the Finger Lakes, and the Niagara River. They are absent from areas near the coast.

Channel catfish prefer the clear water of large rivers and deep lakes. Like most catfish, they tolerate poorer conditions, though not to the same degree as bullheads. They tend to hide in deep, dark pools or under debris in the daylight hours and become more active toward dusk and after dark. Unlike most other catfish, they may thrive in fast river currents. They use their good sense of smell and long, sensitive barbels to find food. Channel catfish are omnivorous and will eat almost anything, including mollusks, crayfish, aquatic insects, worms, and fish, and may even scavenge on dead fish and animals. They also eat algae and aquatic plants.

Channel catfish can reach more than 20 pounds and to catch one near 10 pounds is not unusual. The North American record is 58 pounds. They are among the most sought-after gamefish in many parts of the United States. They are not as popular to anglers in the Northeast, mostly because they are not found everywhere and their populations are not concentrated. Where they exist, you can catch them on almost any live bait, and even some stinky commercial baits that take advantage of their smell-feeding abilities. They are great eating and are farm-raised and sold commercially around the United States.

Tadpole Madtom

NOTORUS GYRINUS

Approximately 5 inches

Tadpole madtoms don't grow much longer than 5 inches. They are somewhat similar in appearance to the bullheads. Their adipose fin is connected to the caudal fin, which is large and uniquely very rounded. As their common name implies, they have a distinctive tadpole shape. They are yellowish brown to brown, darkest on their dorsal surface, and gradually becoming lighter on the sides, with a white to yellow belly. They have a dark streak along their lateral line. The four barbels on their upper jaw are dark-colored and the four on their lower jaw are light, sometimes even white. They have the characteristic spines in their dorsal and pectoral fins, which can give a careless angler a painful puncture.

Tadpole madtoms are found in much of the eastern half of the United States. They are not common anywhere in the Northeast, but are found in Connecticut, much of New York State, and here and there in southern New England. They were introduced in many places. They are a popular species for freshwater fish tanks and sometimes are released into locations where they were not previously found.

They live in streams, shallow ponds, swamps, and marshes. They shy away from currents and hide in the weeds and under rocks and logs of a muddy bottom. Tadpole madtoms are nocturnal feeders, for the most part. They are predators, but being so small, they feed mostly on insect larvae and nymphs, small crustaceans, and any other animals small enough for them to swallow. In turn, they become prey to larger fish such as bass, yellow perch, walleye, and even trout.

Because they are so small, the easiest way to catch them is using a dip net or seine. However, they can be caught on a line with a small hook and a small amount of bait.

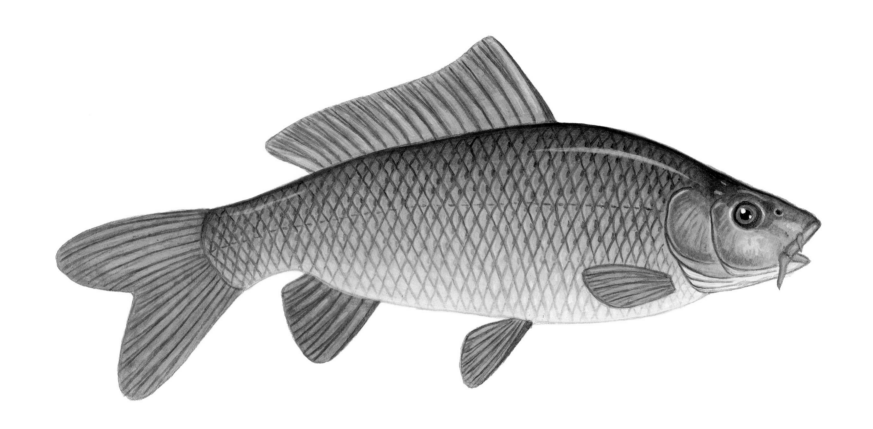

Common Carp

CYPRINUS CARPIO

12–24 inches (1–2 feet)

Carp are large fish, yet they are actually members of the minnow family. They most often are yellow-brown with darker olive-green on the dorsal surface and a light yellow belly. Two small barbels are located on each side of the mouth, which points slightly downward, indicating their bottom-feeding habits. They are omnivorous smell feeders, with a diet that includes insects, crayfish, worms, mollusks, algae, seeds and other plant life in the water. They even scavenge on dead fish.

Common carp are native to Europe and Asia. In the 1870s, the newly established United States Fishing Commission sponsored the stocking of common carp across the United States as a potential food fish and gamefish. They became briefly popular in some restaurants in the United States. However, the increase in ocean fishing and the pollution of many of the nation's larger rivers led to a decline of carp as a food source. As it turns out, their introduction has had negative environmental consequences for a number of reasons. They are now considered an invasive species, with their populations getting out of control in some localities. They affect the vegetation and other fish species by dredging and uprooting plant life on the bottom, altering the water's ecosystem. They even feed on the eggs of other species of fish as they grub around the bottom.

Common carp may be a menace to other fish populations, but you have to admire their ability to survive. In the early 1900s, as industrial wastes increasingly polluted rivers across the United States, carp were able to survive and even thrive despite the warmer water and low oxygen levels, while other species simply died out. As water quality has improved since the 1970s and clean-water species have returned, carp have remained as well.

Despite this negative history in the United States, many anglers treat carp as a major gamefish. The reasons are simple: Carp are found all over the United States (even in big cities), they can grow to well over 25 pounds, and they are good fighters. The bait used for carp can range widely, from corn or a piece of potato to commercial carp concoctions. Some anglers actually fly-fish for them. Hooking into a 10- to 30-pound carp using freshwater fishing gear can be very exciting.

Common Shiner

NOTROPIS CORNUTUS

Approximately 4 inches

Common shiners probably are best known to anglers as a bait-fish for catching predatory fish such as bass, pickerel, and salmon. They live up to their name, with their silvery sides and shiny scales. These scales are unique in that they are taller than they are wide, making for an attractive and flashy bait. The dorsal surface is darker than the sides.

Common shiners prefer rivers and brooks but are also found in lakes and ponds throughout the Northeast and beyond, in both cool and warm water, as long as the water is clean. They feed on insects, insect larvae, worms, and small fish. Their mouths are fairly large and horizontal, adapted for feeding at and just below the water's surface. You can see them from time to time snapping at insects on the surface, particularly at dusk. They are often found in schools.

They provide good forage in lakes and rivers for gamefish and are an important part of the ecosystem. They are in the minnow family, averaging less than 4 inches in length, but can grow to about 8 inches. It is possible to catch them on a fishing line, but they are more often caught in nets and traps and used as live bait. They are sold in bait stores throughout the region year-round.

While fishing in northern Maine several years ago, just before canoeing from a small inlet out into a large lake, we spent a few minutes catching small common shiners to use for bait. We were able to capture about fifteen shiners with a piece of worm on a small hook. Never having fished there before, we wondered whether they would be effective for catching the salmon out in the main part of the lake. About an hour later, we had our answer. I caught a 25-inch Atlantic salmon using one of the shiners. When I cleaned the salmon to grill for lunch, I found its stomach stuffed with six common shiners exactly the same size as the one I used to catch the salmon. We certainly were using the right bait that morning.

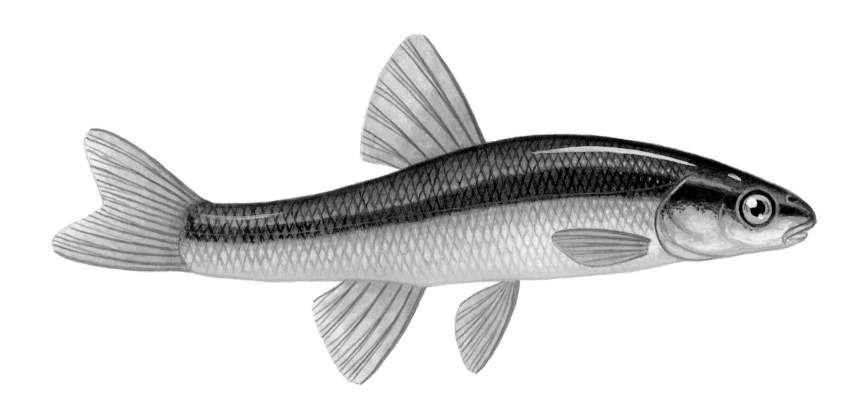

Blacknose Dace

RHINICHTHYS ATRATULUS

Approximately 3 inches

Blacknose dace look similar to longnose dace. However, the snout on blacknose dace protrudes only slightly beyond the lower jaw, while the longnose dace's snout protrudes well beyond the lower jaw. Blacknose dace have a barbel near the hinge of the mouth on each side. They have very small scales that are difficult to see and give the fish a smooth look. Blacknose dace generally are brown on the dorsal surface, becoming somewhat lighter brownish yellow to grey on the sides, sometimes with irregularly shaped specks throughout. The belly is silvery white. A dark band along the sides passing through the eye to the tip of the snout distinguishes blacknose dace from longnose dace and other similar minnows. Blacknose dace are relatively slender minnows that only grow to about 3 inches in length.

Blacknose dace inhabit small, clear, fast-moving streams. They frequently are found in the same sort of habitat as longnose dace and brook trout. Blacknose dace normally are not found in lakes or ponds. They feed on most tiny invertebrates, including insect larvae and worms, as well as algae. Blacknose dace spawn in the late spring to early summer. Females deposit about 750 eggs in a gravel nest, males fertilize the eggs, and both abandon the nest site and leave the young to develop on their own.

They are not commonly sold or sought after as baitfish, most likely because they do not have the silvery shine of other popular baitfish and are somewhat dull in color. However, blacknose dace certainly can be used for bait and can be caught easily in a minnow trap or with a dip net.

Longnose Dace

RHINICHTHYS CATARACTAE

3–4 inches

Longnose dace look similar to blacknose dace, but have a snout that extends well beyond the lower jaw, accounting for their name. Longnose dace have a barbel near the hinge of the jaw on each side. The body is rounded and rather stout. They can grow up to 6 inches long but average 3 to 4 inches. They are darkest on top, with an overall blotchy olive-green color on the sides, becoming lighter or even white on the belly.

Longnose dace prefer the cold, fast water of streams and often are found in the same kind of brooks and streams as brook trout. Individuals that live in lakes spend much of their time in the areas where the waves break and the water is moving. They feed on most small invertebrates but particularly small crustaceans, insect larvae, and worms, as well as algae.

Longnose dace sometimes are used as a baitfish but are not widely sold for that purpose. Catching one in the place where you are fishing and using it as bait is a good idea. This way, you are using natural bait and not introducing a new species into a body of water where it did not previously exist. They keep fairly well after capture.

A pattern of dark dorsal and light ventral surfaces, called countershading, is typical in most fish and serves as a basic form of camouflage. The dark dorsal surface blends into the dark bottom when viewed from above, while the lighter belly blends into the light from the surface when viewed from below. Predators on the same level as their potential prey see a less conspicuous profile than would ordinarily be created by light and shadow. A dark line or band on the sides often breaks up the shape of a prey fish, also acting as a form of protective coloration.

Northern Redbelly Dace

PHOXINUS EOS

2–3 inches

Northern redbelly dace are somewhat rounded and stout, but slender-looking viewed from the side. They have pointed heads and no barbels. Their backs most often are dark olive-brown, becoming silvery cream on the sides, with two dark bands running along the sides from the tail to the snout. The bands are somewhat broken as they pass through the operculum and the snout. The upper band is located between the mid-lateral side and the upper dorsal surface and is usually less prominent. The sides below the bands become bright red in breeding males, lending this fish its common name. The males have yellow fins during spawning time in the late spring into the summer as well. They are very nice-looking fish during this time.

Northern redbelly dace are found throughout the Northeast. Their range extends through much of the eastern and central United States up into Canada, including Quebec, Nova Scotia, and Prince Edward Island. They tend to inhabit small streams but sometimes are found in small ponds. They favor slow-moving pools, but sometimes are found in moderate currents. These dace also seem to prefer being among weeds if they are available. They can be found in acidic, tea-colored water near bogs or swamps, particularly in some of the more northern portions of the Northeast.

Northern redbelly dace eat small invertebrates, filamentous green algae, and even other tiny fish. They tend to eat more vegetation than most dace species. They can be trapped and used for bait where they are locally abundant but are not commonly used for this purpose.

Fallfish

SEMOTILUS CORPORALIS

6–9 inches

Fallfish are the largest native members of the minnow family in the Northeast, and resemble other minnows. Fallfish sometimes are confused with shiners, especially small individuals. As they grow larger, they develop a more rounded body shape and distinctive look. They have a shiny, silvery body with a bit of a darkened background color. This darkness is largely caused by a unique characteristic in fallfish: Their large scales are outlined in dark brown, creating a look of chicken wire on their sides. The dorsal surface is dark brown or black, and the belly is white. Males sometimes have a pinkish tint to their body during spawning season, usually in late spring.

Fallfish prefer cool, clean rivers and streams and are found less often in ponds and lakes. When they are young, they inhabit the rocky swirls of a fast-moving current. As they mature, they prefer deeper, slow-moving water. They frequent the same habitats as trout, and sometimes are mistaken for a trout on the line.

Fallfish put up a terrific fight for a minnow. They can grow to over 3 pounds and be up to 18 or 20 inches in length, although they average only 6 to 9 inches. Fallfish generally are not sought as a gamefish, and are not very good to eat, but they are fun to catch, and give you a bit of a thrill until you realize they are not a trout. They are more often used as live bait for catching large trout, salmon, and bass.

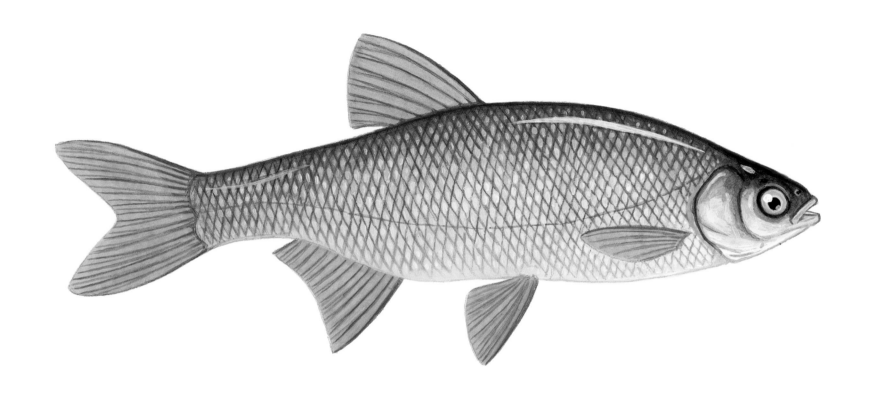

Golden Shiner

NOTEMIGONUS CRYSOLEUCAS

3–6 inches

olden shiners have a deep body, yet it is compressed and rather thin. They have a small mouth and a small pointed head. Adults live up to their name, with their golden, silvery sides. They are darkest on the dorsal surface and more silvery on the belly. They often have red-orange fins, but this is particularly true in males during spawning season. Another distinctive characteristic is their curved lateral lines, which start just behind the upper region of the operculum, dip deeply in the middle, and curve up to the end of the tail. They also have a unique scaleless strip from the back of the pelvic fin to the anus. Occasionally, they can grow to more than 12 inches in length.

Golden shiners are found in most slow-moving rivers and streams as well as ponds and lakes throughout the Northeast. They are native to the Northeast up into Canada and down the East Coast to Florida. Golden shiners also have made their way westward, mostly by introduction as a forage fish or by their wide use as a baitfish. They prefer clean, cool water with an abundance of aquatic vegetation.

Golden shiners spawn over an extended period of time from late spring to the middle of the summer. Females deposit eggs in the gravel and aquatic vegetation of the shallow water. They normally abandon their eggs after spawning and do not guard them themselves, but females sometimes deposit their eggs in the nests of other fish such as sunfish and then let the male sunfish guard the eggs with its own.

Golden shiners feed on a variety of foods, including insects, insect larvae and nymphs, small mollusks, small fish, and even aquatic plant life. They will take bait and flies quite easily, but anglers don't seek to catch them except as a baitfish. They may be caught in a minnow trap as bait for trout, salmon, bass, pike, chain pickerel, and a number of other game-fish. They are often the preferred bait-fish because they stay alive so well. Kids would have fun fishing for them, as they are relatively easy to catch.

Fish that school seem to swim as if they were one organism. They are able to accomplish this mostly due to their lateral lines, visible along their sides, which act as an extra sense organ in fish. Lateral lines actually are a series of pores leading to a water-filled canal on each side lined with nerve receptors. Lateral lines provide a sense of touch at a distance, allowing fish to detect vibrations and sounds as well as pressure exerted by other fish around them, aiding them in finding prey or avoiding predators, and helping them to coordinate their movements in the school. Fish toward the edges of the school must rely on other senses such as sight; they are constantly trying to keep up with the school from behind.

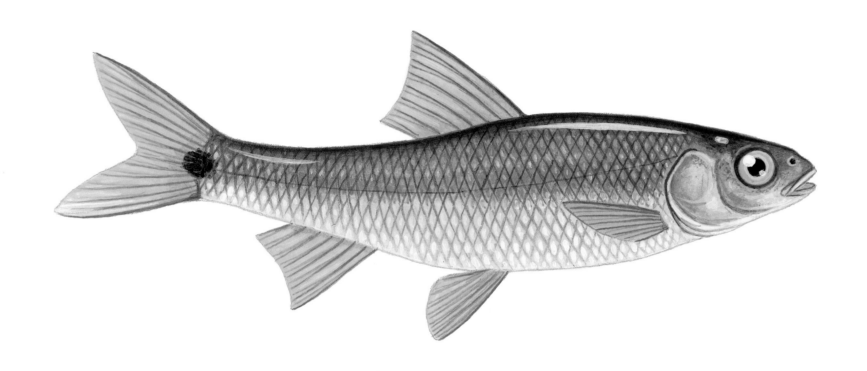

Spottail Shiner

NOTROPIS HUDSONIUS

4–6 inches

Spottail shiners look somewhat similar to common shiners, but they have a dark spot in the middle of the tail at the base of the caudal fin that distinguishes them from other shiners and minnows. The body is narrow but a bit rounded and particularly blunt in the head. They have large eyes, and a rather small, horizontal to slightly upward-pointing mouth. The dorsal and anal fins often have a concave, crescent-shaped curve on the outer posterior margins that helps identify the spottail shiner. Like most shiners, the sides and belly are silvery, and the dorsal surface is just slightly darker olive-brown to bluish grey.

Spottail shiners are common throughout much of the Northeast and beyond, where they inhabit large lakes and rivers as well as small ponds and streams. They seem to do best in clean, clear water.

The spottail shiner is a very important forage fish for larger gamefish. They have that shiny look that makes them good baitfish, though their scales tend to flake off when you handle them.

You can hook a shiner for bait several ways. If you are going to troll slowly or just cast and retrieve your bait, put the hook through the bottom lip first and pull it straight up through the top lip. This way, the shiner stays upright, and the hook is facing the direction of the retrieve, so when a fish strikes, it can be hooked easily. If you are bobber fishing or just casting out to let the shiner sink to the bottom, hook it through the upper back or the tail. Try to put the hook below the spinal cord so as not to harm the fish too badly, so it will be able to swim and move, attracting the attention of larger fish. Gamefish usually swallow a fish headfirst, so the hook will be facing in the opposite direction and will engage easily.

Creek Chub

SEMOTILUS ATROMACULATUS

6–12 inches

Creek chub are very thick and "chubby" little fish. They are most round and stout toward the anterior end and narrow a bit toward the tail. The big, blunt head has a large mouth, with a flap-like barbel at the hinge on each side of the jaw. They have very tiny scales. They are olive-brown on the dorsal surface, becoming silvery gray on the sides, sometimes with a purplish tint. The belly is creamy white, though males' bellies may become rosy during breeding season. Some individuals have an indistinct dark stripe along the mid-lateral sides that becomes less prominent as they get older. The best mark to distinguish creek chub from other minnows is a dark spot at the lower anterior end of the dorsal fin.

As the name suggests, creek chub favor the deeper pools of streams and small brooks, but they can be found in the shallows of small, gravel-bottomed lakes and ponds. Their range covers most of the central and eastern United States, excluding Florida, north to Maine and into Canada. Creek chub eat surface insects as well as insect larvae and nymphs. Larger creek chub are capable of eating other small fish, crayfish, small mollusks, and worms. Spawning takes place from mid- to late spring in most locations. Males build a nest in the pebbles and gravelly bottom of streams in a quiet pool. After the females spawn, the males fertilize and cover the eggs with gravel, then guard the nest from potential predators until the eggs hatch.

Despite being a minnow, creek chub sometimes can grow to 12 inches long. They can be caught easily on a fishing line and often are caught by fishermen fly-fishing for trout. They are caught easily in minnow traps and seines, or you can catch them with a small hook and a piece of worm. They are very popular as baitfish in some areas. Because of their heftiness, they tend to cast out further than other baitfish of the same length. This gets your bait out where the bigger fish are waiting for a chubby snack. Lures have been modeled and named after the creek chub.

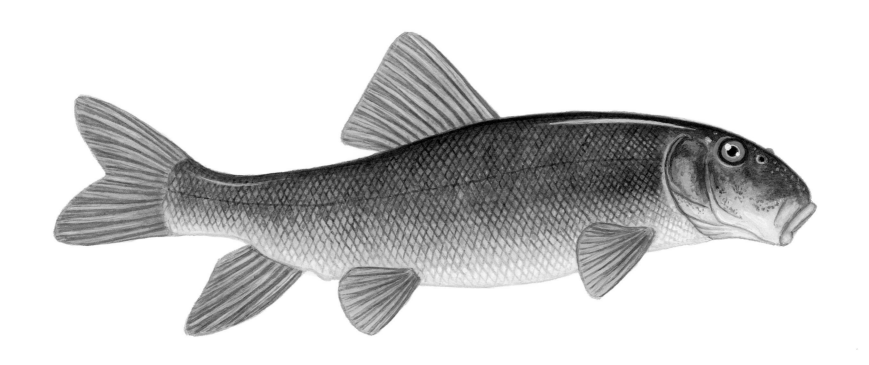

White Sucker

CATOSTOMUS COMMERSONII

10–18 inches

I remember once fishing with my father in a brook near our camp in western Massachusetts when I was about fourteen years old. This brook had occasional fast water but also had some sharp bends where the water slowed down into deep, boulder-filled pools. In the past, we had caught only average-sized brook trout in this location. However, we had heard stories of an occasional large brown trout taken there. On this day, my father hooked into a large fish while sitting on a boulder overlooking a bend in the brook. He started yelling for me to run to the car and get the net that we had left there inadvertently. I could see his rod bending almost in half and the water swirling in the deep, dark pool. I ran as fast as I could, through some hemlocks, and up the 50-foot embankment to the dirt road and the car. I grabbed the net and ran back down, almost tripping and falling along the way, just in time to lean over the big rock and net the large fish. To our surprise, it was not a trout at all. It was a very large white sucker. I was so winded as we started laughing out of control. I often wondered whether it could have been any more exciting if it really had been a large trout. I think this time it really didn't matter.

White suckers have soft fins, blunt and rounded heads, and cylinder-shaped bodies. They have no scales on their heads, but the rest of their body is covered with visible scales. They are slow-moving for the most part and spend much of the time feeding on the bottom.

White suckers are found in most rivers, brooks, and lakes throughout the Northeast and much of the rest of North America. They tolerate a wide range of water conditions, including warm water and low oxygen levels. Their success can be attributed to their omnivorous feeding habits. Their mouths and rubbery lips turn downward to suck insect larvae and nymphs, tiny clams and snails, crustaceans, worms, and even small amounts of algae from the bottom. They wedge into crevices between rocks, sucking and scraping for insect nymphs firmly attached to the rocks.

White suckers usually are not fished as a food source, although some say they are good eating. Usually they are caught while baitfishing on the bottom for gamefish such as trout. They are not that easy to catch on purpose, but when you do, they can put up a pretty good fight. Young ones often are used as live baitfish.

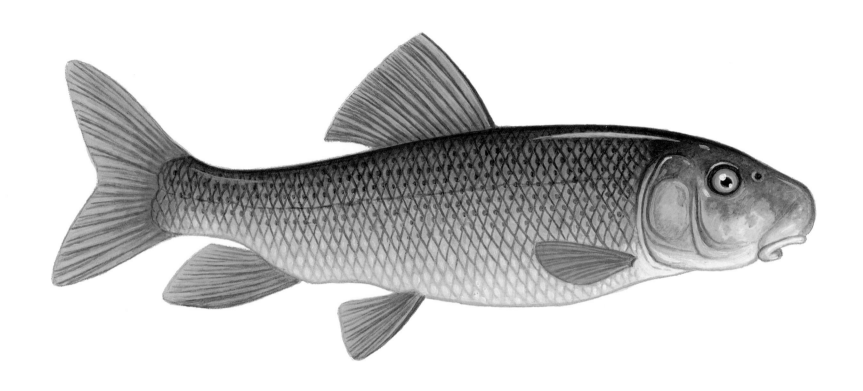

Greater Redhorse

MOXOSTOMA VALENCIENNESI

Approximately 18 inches

Greater redhorse are rather good-looking for a sucker. They have a stout, rounded body, a blunt head, and a large, ventrally located mouth. They are light olive on the dorsal surface and silvery on the sides, sometimes with an orange or copper tint. Each very large scale has a dark area at its base, giving the fish a textured look. The fins are often red to orange. Greater redhorse frequently are confused with other redhorse species such as river redhorse, but they may be distinguished by their rounded, fan-like dorsal fins. Other similar species have slightly concave dorsal fins.

In the Northeast, greater redhorse are found only in Vermont and New York. They are not numerous anywhere but are found in the north-central United States around the Great Lakes up to Canada's Hudson Bay, Ontario, Quebec, and down into the Saint Lawrence River drainage. They most often are found in moderate to large rivers and sometimes in large lakes. They seem to favor medium-fast currents, but may spend time in deep, quiet pools. They prefer rivers with a gravel bottom and boulders.

Greater redhorse feed on crustaceans, small mollusks, and insect larvae and nymphs, and may consume algae and plant debris. They use molar-like teeth in the back of their throats to crush small clams, a large part of their diet in some locations.

Greater redhorse populations may have diminished. Limited studies have been conducted on this fish, but they seem to be sensitive to some human activities. Greater redhorse spawn up rivers where the water is shallow and the bottom is gravelly. They sometimes need to travel long distances to get to these spawning places. Many rivers now have dams, and culverts make it difficult for fish to pass under some roads, blocking the way to the best spawning areas. This may not completely stop them from spawning, but can reduce the number of offspring produced.

Anglers who happen to hook into a large greater redhorse may be in for a surprisingly fierce battle. Worms, small crayfish, or mealworms are considered good baits. Greater redhorse are edible and some anglers seek them out for this purpose.

Creek Chubsucker

ERIMYZON OBLONGUS

6–10 inches

Creek chubsuckers have rather cylindrical bodies with sucker-type mouths situated a little less ventrally than most other sucker species, causing some to confuse chubsuckers with shiner species. They usually are olive on the dorsal surface and lighter yellowish golden on the sides, with a dark band along the lateral line. The belly is yellow to white. The scales have dark edges, giving creek chubsuckers a mottled look. Adults may have very faint vertical bars, mainly toward the dorsal surface.

Creek chubsuckers are common in a large part of the eastern half of the United States and are native to most of the regions they inhabit. They can be found in ponds or lakes, but appear to favor clear, slow-moving rivers and streams with abundant amounts of vegetation. They prefer bodies of water with gravelly or sandy bottoms.

Creek chubsuckers feed mostly on small invertebrates. Their diet includes crustaceans, clams, aquatic insects, insect larvae and nymphs, and algae. They spawn in the spring on gravel or sand bottom. This usually happens in reduced current, where the stream has slowed into a quiet pool. Males may contribute to digging out a depression in the sand or gravel for the female to spawn or they may use depressions made previously by other species. Females sometimes dig their snouts into the gravel, which seems to be a signal that they are about to spawn. Eggs number in the thousands.

Creek chubsuckers are used widely as baitfish in the areas they inhabit. Their rounded shape, chunkiness, and golden shininess make them effective as bait. They are quite hardy to keep in a bucket and last a long time on the fishing line. They can be captured using a minnow trap or small seine.

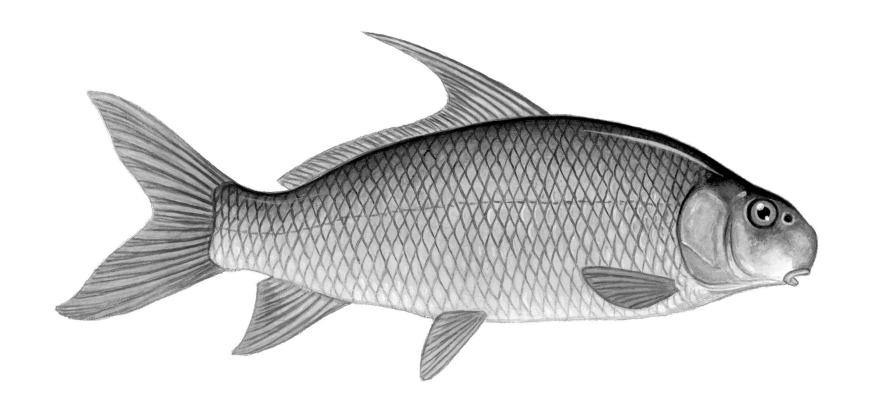

Quillback

CARPIODES CYPRINUS

15–20 inches

Quillbacks are unusual-looking fish. They sometimes are called carpsuckers because they look like carp but have the downward-pointing mouth and lips of a sucker. In fact, they are in the sucker family. They lack the barbels found on carp. They have large, silvery to slightly bronze scales on their sides, a grayish dorsal surface, and a white belly. They have an arched back and a forked caudal fin. The anterior end of the dorsal fin is very long and pointed like a quill, giving quillbacks their name and an appearance unlike any other sucker.

Quillbacks are not widely found in the Northeast. They inhabit a few of the bigger rivers and lakes around the region. However, they are fairly common in Lake Erie and the other Great Lakes, in the Saint Lawrence River, and in Lake Champlain. They prefer medium-deep water, usually about 15 to 25 feet. In rivers, they seek slow-moving, deep pools. They feed on small crustaceans, insect larvae and nymphs, and tiny freshwater clams. They may even feed on aquatic algae.

They can grow to 20 inches or more as adults and weigh over 10 pounds. As small fish, they are an important source of forage for larger gamefish. Like their relatives, quillbacks are edible but very bony and not that desirable to most anglers. In the Northeast, they are not sought after as a food source by humans. They are not easy to catch, even if you had a desire to do so.

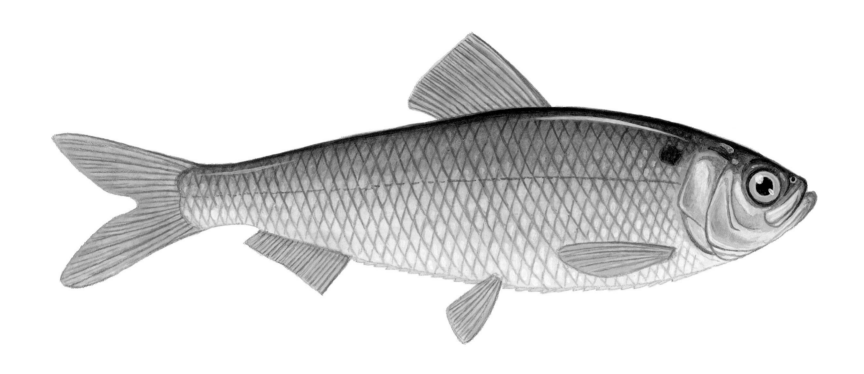

Alewife

ALOSA PSEUDOHARENGUS

7–10 inches

Alewives most closely resemble blueback herring, a relative also found in the Northeast. Alewives have a similar, herring-shaped body, with serrations along their ventral ridges. Both have strongly forked caudal fins and no spines in their fins. Alewives have deeper bodies than blueback and other herring. They also have a distinctive dark spot behind their eyes, just beyond the operculum. Uniquely in alewives, the distance between the eye and the most anterior point of their jaw is equal to the diameter of their large eye. They are darkest on their grayish green dorsal surface and quite silvery on the sides of their compressed body, with a white belly.

Alewives are native to rivers and tributaries along the Atlantic coast from Newfoundland to the Carolinas. They spend most of their lives in the ocean, but travel up these rivers and streams in the late spring to spawn. Like many other anadromous fish, they have been introduced into inland bodies of water throughout the Northeast and have become landlocked. They may have made their way into the Great Lakes by inadvertent or intentional stockings. Another theory is that they entered through the Welland Canal that creates a bypass around Niagara Falls, in effect connecting the Saint Lawrence River and the Atlantic Ocean to the Great Lakes. Although alewives have become forage for larger gamefish, their impact may be more negative than positive in most locations, because they feed on the fry of native species and compete with them for food.

Alewives are edible, but they were more popular in the past, when smoked or salted alewives were a common dish. They usually don't grow very large, only reaching 7 or 8 inches in landlocked conditions, although marine individuals sometimes can reach 12 inches. They now are used largely as bait, both on the hook and in lobster traps along the New England coast.

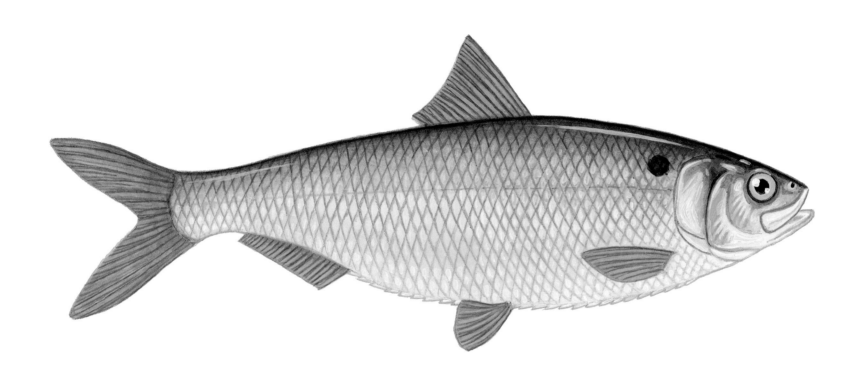

Blueback Herring

ALOSA AESTIVALIS

Approximately 10 inches

Blueback herring are similar to alewives in general shape and look, but bluebacks have smaller eyes. As the name suggests, blueback herring have a dark bluish dorsal surface, becoming silvery on the sides and lightest on the belly. Both blueback herring and alewives have visible ventral serrations. The blueback herring has rather large scales and a dark spot posterior and slightly dorsal to the operculum. The caudal fin is deeply forked. The lower jaw projects beyond the upper jaw and the mouth points upward. Bluebacks can grow to 16 inches, but landlocked freshwater individuals are smaller.

Blueback herring are anadromous, but some populations have become landlocked in inland lakes along the East Coast. The ocean-dwelling members are found from Nova Scotia to Florida. Most freshwater populations were introduced as a result of fishermen using them for bait and releasing the unused fish into the water where they were fishing. In the past, they may have been stocked as forage for larger gamefish, but their introduction has caused more problems than benefit. They compete for food with young gamefish and eat other fishes' eggs, including the eggs of largemouth bass. Many states now have restrictions on using blueback herring as bait in freshwater lakes and rivers unless they already exist there. Their diet also includes aquatic insects, surface insects, and small fish.

Blueback herring spawn in the spring, a bit later than alewives, when the water is warmer. The fertilized eggs are denser than the water and sticky, so they adhere to the gravel and rocks on the bottom of the stream. After hatching, the young spend very little time in their natal streams and rivers before making their way to the ocean.

Herring were more popular in the years before refrigeration, when they were salted and stored for later consumption. With the ability to refrigerate and freeze fish, more popular fish species became easy to keep and store. Today, blueback herring are still eaten and loved by some, but much of the catch is used for bait or made into pet food.

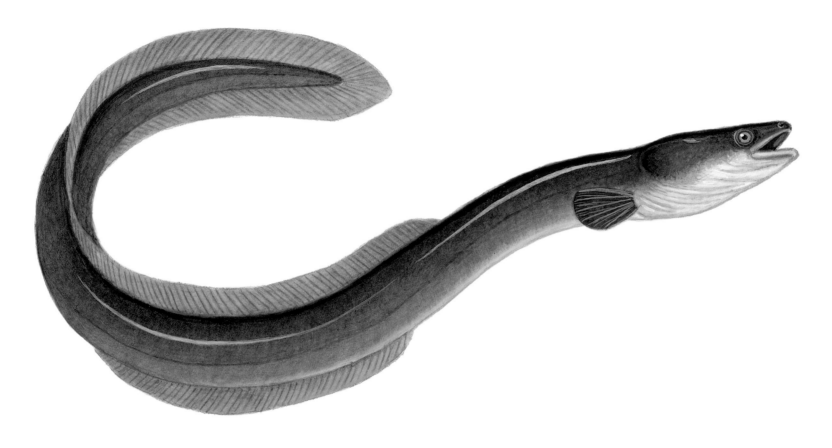

American Eel

ANGUILLA ROSTRATA

24–36 inches (2–3 feet)

American eels are not like any other bony fish in North America. They are almost snake-like in appearance. They have true jaws and paired pectoral fins but have no pelvic fins. These characteristics distinguish them from sea lamprey, a primitive jawless fish, and the only fish that could be confused with the American eel. American eels are olive-brown except on the belly, which is light yellow to white. They have no scales and have very smooth, slimy skin. Females grow larger than males, sometimes reaching a length of 5 feet, while males are usually only 2 to 3 feet long.

American eels are catadromous fish. After between five and thirty years in freshwater, adult eels make their way back to the ocean, to where they were born in the Sargasso Sea, between the West Indies and Bermuda. Here, individuals from wide-ranging breeding populations gather for spawning and then die. Their eggs are less dense than the salt water and float to the surface before hatching. The semi-transparent larvae drift with the ocean currents toward the mainland. The larval eels now swim up virtually every freshwater river and stream from northern portions of South America, northward along the entire east coast of North America, to as far north as Greenland and Iceland. Females tend to migrate farther up rivers and spend much more time in freshwater than do males.

Their diets are wide ranging. They feed on everything from insect larvae and nymphs, to small fish, crayfish, aquatic salamanders, and even dead fish and other decaying animals.

Eels are able to take in oxygen through their skin to supplement their gills, allowing them to crawl through damp areas to journey from one water body to another. With this ability to squirm and crawl, they can make their way beyond rivers and streams to ponds and lakes.

Some Asians and Europeans consider eels very desirable eating fish, but they are not consumed widely in the United States. They are harvested for bait to catch striped bass and bluefish in the Northeast. They generally are not sought after by fishermen but provide an unusual surprise when you reel one in.

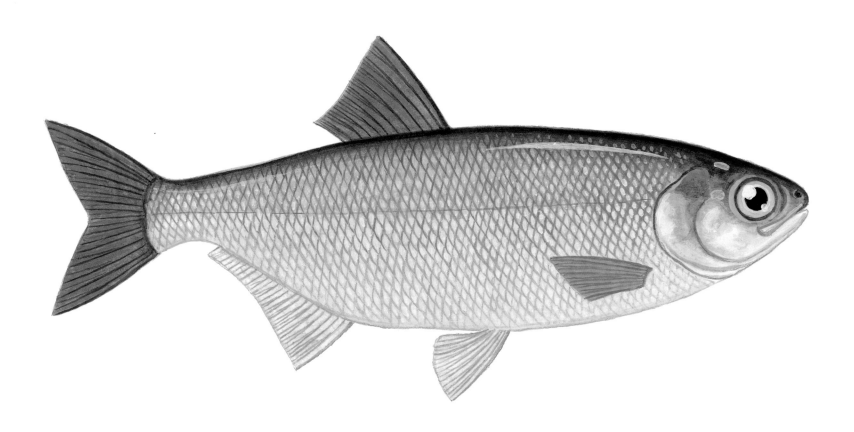

Mooneye

HIODON TERGISUS

10–16 inches

Mooneyes are light-colored fish with large, silvery eyes, rather small, short heads, and flattened bodies. Their mouths are fairly large for the size of the head, with the hinge of the mouth extending to below the pupil of the eye. Mooneyes are unique in having teeth on their tongues and the roof of the mouth. They are slightly dark greenish blue on the dorsal surface and silver to white on the sides and belly. The dorsal fin starts before the beginning of the anal fin, which distinguishes mooneyes from their closest relative, the goldeyes, which are the only other fish in this genus in North America.

In the Northeast, mooneyes are found in Lake Champlain in Vermont and New York, in the Saint Lawrence River drainage, in Lake Erie, and in the other Great Lakes (except Lake Superior). They also inhabit a scattering of other rivers and lakes throughout New York. They tend to favor the clean, clear water of rivers and large streams and often are found in the faster currents. They migrate into the rocky, fast water of rivers to spawn. Their eggs sometimes are covered in a gelatin-like material, similar to frogs and other amphibians. Mooneyes live for ten to twelve years and can weigh 10 to 12 pounds.

Their mouths point upward, indicating their tendency to surface feed, where they gobble up flying insects that fall or land in the water. However, they also feed on crustaceans, mollusks, aquatic insects, and small fish.

Mooneyes are sought by anglers for their energetic fighting rather than for their edibility. As surface feeders, they can be taken on dry and wet flies near the surface, or with any live bait you would use for sunfish or bass.

Bowfin

AMIA CALVA

18–24 inches

Bowfin have large, scaleless heads with a huge mouth and small, but very sharp teeth. A distinctive barbel is located at each nostril. They are a rather mottled, dark olive-green on the dorsal surface, lighter toward the ventral surface, with light cream to light green bellies. The fins on spawning males often turn almost turquoise. A distinctive dark spot on each side of the dorsal part of the tail becomes less prominent as the fish grow older. The dorsal fin runs more than half the length of the body and the caudal fin is very rounded. The body is very long and stout and is covered with scales everywhere but the head.

Bowfin are very large, unusual fish that haven't changed much in over a hundred million years, an indication of how well adapted they are for where they live. Bowfin usually inhabit rather shallow water with lots of weeds. They favor the coves and inlets of rivers, lakes, and ponds. They can survive in water with low oxygen much better than most fish, largely due to their ability to gulp air into the air bladder as a supplement to their gill breathing. Bowfin can grow to over 2 feet and weigh 5 or 6 pounds, sometimes even more.

Bowfin are found in much of the eastern half of the United States except along the Appalachian Mountains. They are not common in the Northeast, but are found in some big lakes such as Lake Champlain and Lake George, as well as in the Saint Lawrence River and much of the Connecticut River. In addition, many populations were started by illegal introductions in reservoirs, ponds, lakes, and rivers throughout New England and New York.

Their diet consists mostly of other fish, but they also feed on frogs, crayfish, and other invertebrates such as leeches and worms. Although some seek out bowfin as sport fish because of their superior fighting ability, they are not sought after on a large scale by anglers. Many people consider them a nuisance and not particularly edible.

Lake Sturgeon

ACIPENSER FULVESCENS

48–72 inches (4–6 feet)

Champ is the name given to the mysterious "sea" monster of Lake Champlain. More than three hundred sightings have been reported over the last three centuries. Like the Loch Ness Monster in Scotland, Champ is thought by some to be a plesiosaur, a prehistoric water-dwelling reptile that somehow escaped extinction and is still living in Lake Champlain. There are a number of blurry photographs, eyewitness accounts, and legendary folk tales about this creature, yet no real concrete evidence has been found of its existence.

The most plausible theory explaining this monster's existence is that it *is* a very large, prehistoric animal—one that is known to still exist, and actually lives in Lake Champlain. This animal is the lake sturgeon. They can grow to 300 pounds and to a length of 8 feet or more. Sturgeon have tough, leathery skin. Five rows of reptile-like, bony plates run along the length of the body: two rows on each side and one along the dorsal surface, giving sturgeon a serrated, prehistoric look.

Their large heads and snout-like mouths, serrated dorsal ridge, and asymmetrical tails match some of the daunting descriptions of the lake creature that supposedly lives in Lake Champlain.

Beyond Lake Champlain, lake sturgeon inhabit other large lakes and rivers in the middle to northern United States, including the Great Lakes and the Saint Lawrence River. They are bottom feeders and tend to spend much of their time in shallow water. They sense the food in the mud and gravel bottom with the very sensitive barbels on their lower jaw and strain out their diet of crayfish, insect larvae, snails, small clams, leeches, and other small animals with their protruding, toothless mouths. Any silt or debris is expelled out through the gills.

Lake sturgeon are very long-lived, averaging seventy years, with a few individuals known to have lived well beyond one hundred years. Females don't even spawn until they are at least twenty years old, and then spawn once every four to seven years. Males are sexually mature at a slightly younger age. Sturgeon spawn between May and June up rivers and large streams, broadcasting their eggs on the gravel bottom. They have been known to leap out of the water and flop back on the surface during the spawning season. Could this be another piece of evidence that Champ is actually a lake sturgeon?

Lake sturgeon are edible and their meat is firm and said to be delicious. Eggs taken from within a female fish are made into the delicacy, caviar. To catch one, you have to fish on the bottom using small bait, such as a night crawler or piece of fish.

Lake sturgeon are considered threatened or endangered in most of the places where they exist. With their slow reproductive habits and long time to reach maturity, combined with years of overfishing, pollution, and dam building on the large rivers they prefer, their once-large numbers are down. Many restrictions control their harvesting in most states where they exist.

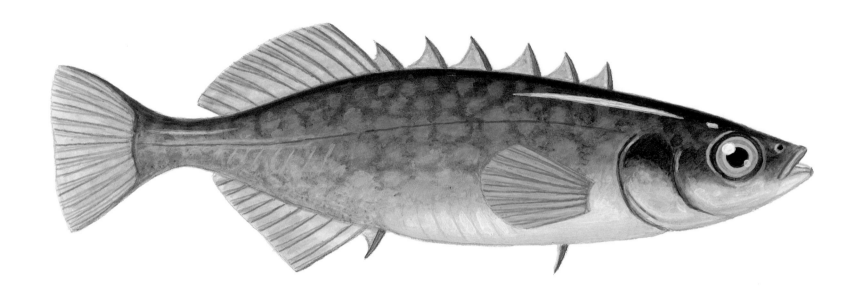

Brook Stickleback

EUCALIA INCONSTANS

Approximately 3 inches

Brook sticklebacks are small fish, with a life span of about three years. They are odd-looking, with five or six bony, rear-pointing dorsal spines in front of the soft, squarish dorsal fin, and another very sharp spine on each pelvic and anal fin. They usually are dark olive-green, mottled with lighter green spots on the sides. The fins often are lighter green or even yellowish and somewhat translucent. The body is compressed and quite long and pointed, with a long, skinny tail ending in a slightly rounded caudal fin. Brook sticklebacks have no scales.

Brook sticklebacks spawn in the late spring and early summer. Females spawn in hollow nests constructed by males using mucus produced in their kidneys, mixed with sticks and vegetation from the stream. Males fertilize the eggs, guard them until they hatch, and then continue to guard the fry for about two weeks.

They inhabit cool, clear, slow-moving rivers and streams, lakes, and ponds. They seem to favor areas with filamentous green algae, which they sometimes eat. They often are found among other minnows. Other times, they are found hiding under embankments and in rocks and debris in the water. Despite their small size, brook sticklebacks can be aggressive predators, feeding on most small aquatic creatures, including insects and crustaceans, insect larvae and nymphs, tiny mollusks, worms, and fish eggs. Despite their spines, other larger fish such as trout, pickerel, bass, and yellow perch prey on them.

In the Northeast, brook sticklebacks are found in Pennsylvania, New York, and all of the New England states except Rhode Island. They are not abundant in any of these places except for parts of New York. Some of the populations in the Northeast may be a result of accidental introductions: Although not widely used for bait, they often end up in bait buckets containing other baitfish and subsequently are thrown into a pond or river. Their wider range includes the north-central United States.

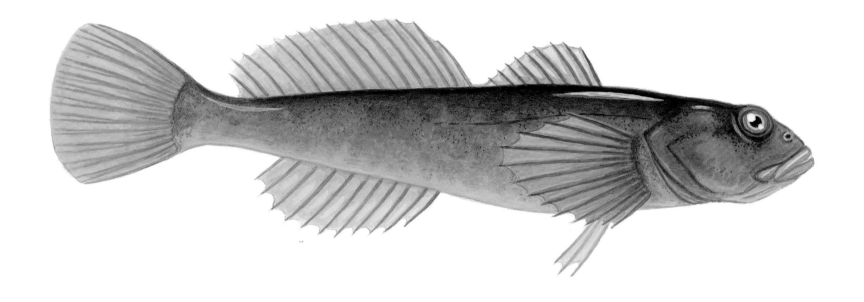

Slimy Sculpin

COTTUS COGNATUS

3–5 inches

Slimy sculpin are small, but they are an unusual-looking fish to find in a river or stream when you are in search of a brook trout. They have no scales. Their heads are quite broad and flat, with no barbels. The eyes are located nearly on top of the head. They have two barely connected dorsal fins. The anterior dorsal fin is small, with spines, while the posterior dorsal fin is long, with rays and no spines. The pectoral fins are very large, fan-like, and distinctive. The caudal fin is slightly rounded. Slimy sculpin are olive-brown, with some lighter mottling on the sides. The belly is much lighter and can have an orange tinge, particularly in males during the spawning season.

Slimy sculpin are found throughout the northeastern United States and into Canada. They occupy inland cold-water streams similar to the habitats where brook trout are found. They also live in lakes. In very large lakes, they have been found at depths well over 100 feet.

Slimy sculpin spawn in the early spring. The males build the nests, usually under an embankment or within some debris. Females lay sticky eggs and males fertilize them, then guard the nest and even the young after they hatch.

They feed on any small invertebrates they can swallow, including tiny aquatic insects, insect nymphs and larvae, and even small fish. They also have been known to feed on fish eggs, including the eggs of brook trout.

Slimy sculpin move in spurts, darting around the bottom somewhat like a darter. Like darters, slimy sculpin have no air bladder, and spend much of their time resting on the bottom. This lack of rapid swimming skills make slimy sculpin easy prey for larger fish, including trout, bass, and even burbot in the deep water of a large lake.

Banded Killifish

FUNDULUS DIAPHANOUS

3–4 inches

Banded killifish have stout, rounded bodies with flat heads and backs. Their bodies are quite long, with a large, slightly rounded caudal fin. They are olive-green on the dorsal surface, becoming lighter and even silvery toward the belly, where the color becomes nearly white. Several vertical bars on the sides are thickest toward the dorsal surface, thinning and disappearing toward the belly. The vertical bars usually are darker and more distinct in females than in males. Banded killifish look similar to striped killifish, but banded killifish tend to have more and narrower vertical bars. They have rather large eyes, and small mouths that turn slightly upward.

Banded killifish are found throughout much of the eastern United States from South Carolina in the south to the Maritime Provinces in the north. They also live west of the Mississippi River to Montana and north through the Great Lakes region and into Ontario. They are found in slow-moving rivers and streams, ponds, lakes, reservoirs, and even the brackish waters of estuaries. They tend to favor sand and gravel bottoms with aquatic plants. In the summer, they also prefer to school in shallow water. They feed on tiny mollusks, crustaceans, various forms of aquatic insects, insect larvae and nymphs, worms, and plant material. Being shallow-water dwellers, they find food on all levels, even though their mouths are adapted for surface feeding.

Banded killifish can grow to about 4 inches and it is possible to hook one on a line with a small hook and a tiny piece of bait. I remember them as a child only because my father used to go out of his way to buy banded killifish at a small bait shop, which sold them as "chubs." They keep much better than most other minnows in a bucket and they last a long time on your line. They are still widely sold as bait in the regions where they exist.

Burbot

LOTA LOTA

Approximately 23 inches

Burbot are the only freshwater member of the cod family, and could not be confused with any other freshwater fish in the Northeast. They have an elongated body that tapers almost to a point toward the tail. They have a wide, flattened head and large mouth with a singe barbel on the lower jaw. The mouth has several rows of small, sharp teeth that point inward. They have extended dorsal and anal fins that run almost half the length of the body, almost reaching the end of the tail. The caudal fin is very rounded. Burbot have dark reddish brown bodies mottled with dark irregular spots, and yellow to whitish bellies. They may appear to be scaleless, but actually have very tiny scales.

Burbot are found in most of the northern third of the United States and most of Canada and into Alaska. They generally are found in deep lakes and large rivers. They are not abundant in the Northeast, but are most common in northern Maine, New Hampshire, Vermont, and upstate New York.

Burbot are aggressive predators. They are slow swimmers and yet are still able to catch their prey. They start out feeding on insect larvae, other small invertebrates, and small fish, but as they get older, they feed almost entirely on other fish. Burbot are primarily night feeders, but anglers occasionally catch them during daylight hours in deep water.

Burbot are truly cold-water fish. They are caught most often in the wintertime through the ice in the Northeast. In the warm summer months, they make their way to the coldest and deepest parts of the lake. Burbot are long-lived and rather slow growers. They don't become sexually mature until they are four or five years old and then spawn in the dead of winter, under the ice.

Catching burbot on purpose is not easy. Anglers catch them sporadically when fishing for lake trout with live bait in deep water. They don't seem to be as active in the summer, but using fresh-cut bait or minnows and fishing deep may bring success. They are not as deep in the winter, and jigging and using minnows and cut bait are the most common methods for catching them through the ice.

Being in the cod family, burbot are considered excellent eating, with flaky, white meat. They can be baked, fried, or used in chowders. The most popular method of cooking is to cut them into bite-sized chunks and boil them. This method firms up the meat and gives it the texture and taste of lobster, delicious dipped in butter. Burbot are best eating when they are around 18 inches or larger.

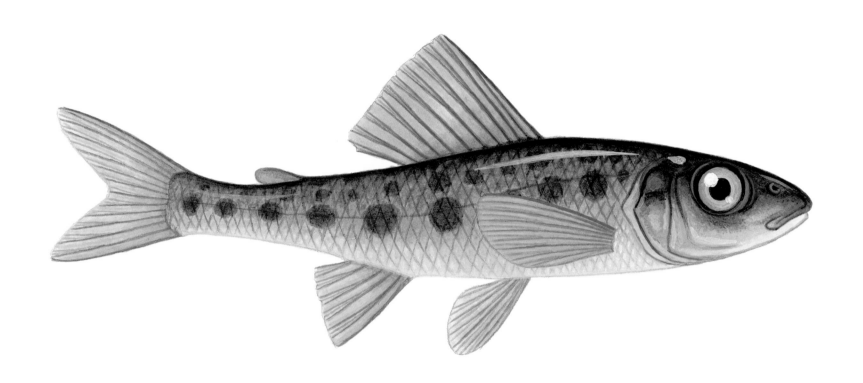

Trout-Perch

PERCOPIS OMISCOMAYCUS

3–5 inches

Trout-perch are neither trout nor perch, although they display characteristics of both. Trout-perch are the only member of a small order of fish that lives in the Northeast. They have an adipose fin like salmon and trout, and the general shape and look of yellow perch. They have large heads, large eyes, and deeply forked caudal fins. They are silvery olive and slightly translucent, with rows of round, dark spots on the back and sides, and nearly white bellies.

Trout-perch favor sandy- or gravelly-bottomed ponds and rivers, with little or no mud, and clean, cool water. They are night feeders, spending most of the daylight hours hiding in debris and deeper water. At night, they travel to shallower water to feed on small aquatic insects, insect larvae, and tiny fish. Trout-perch are a good forage species for larger fish such as walleye, pike, and lake trout.

Trout-perch spawn at night in the late spring or early summer, in the sandy and rocky shallows of the rivers and lakes. Their rather large eggs stick to the rocks and debris and hatch in about a week.

Trout-perch are found in much of the northern half of the United States and Canada, and up into Alaska. They inhabit some lakes and rivers in New York, Vermont, and New Hampshire. They are rather scarce elsewhere in the Northeast, but are found here and there in ponds and streams. Because they are sought after for freshwater fish tanks, they sometimes are released into new habitats, which may account for their existence in some locations.

Given their small size, trout-perch are not a gamefish, but they certainly are an interesting little fish. Because they are not often caught on a fishing line, they are not very well known.

Longnose Gar

LEPISOSTEUS OSSEUS

24–72 inches (2–6 feet)

Longnose gar are long and slender, with unique mouths and jaws that become narrow, with very sharp, protruding teeth. They are distinctive in shape and quite menacing-looking for a freshwater fish in the Northeast. They are olive-brown, darkest on the dorsal surface and becoming lighter toward the belly. They have irregularly shaped dark spots in a row on their sides and scattered on their fins. They have a single dorsal fin and a large, asymmetrical, rounded caudal fin. Their scales are large and coarse, adding to their interesting appearance. They can grow quite large, frequently reaching weights well over 10 pounds. The world record gar was over 50 pounds and was caught in Texas.

Longnose gar favor weedy, shallow water with plenty of logs and debris. They can live in water with lower oxygen levels because of the unusual ability to gulp air into their air bladder and use it to remove oxygen like a lung. Longnose gar haven't changed much in over fifty million years, indicating how well adapted they are for their habitat.

Longnose gar are found in the entire eastern half of the United States, excluding the coastal New England states. They are found in Lake Champlain in Vermont and New York and other large lakes in New York State, as well in the Saint Lawrence and Niagara rivers. They are not found in other parts of the Northeast unless they have been introduced.

Longnose gar are vicious predators. They feed mostly on other fish, grasping their prey sideways with their large mouth and sharp teeth and working it around to swallow it head first. They often are seen resting motionless like a floating branch near the surface, waiting for an ill-fated victim to swim by.

Longnose gar are not popular as gamefish, as they are not very good eating and difficult to clean, but some anglers seek them out using large minnows or artificial lures as bait. The problem is that their sharp teeth often shreds the strongest line or even steel leaders. If a gar strikes when an angler is fishing for other species, it may break the line, causing the loss of an expensive bass plug or lure. They are more popular with bow-fisherman where it is legal to use bows.

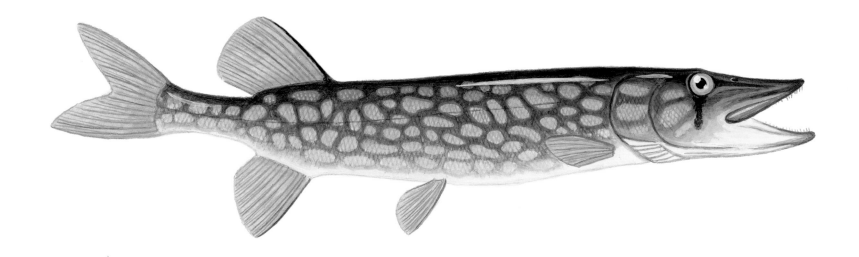

Chain Pickerel

ESOX NIGER

10–16 inches

Chain pickerel look similar to redfin pickerel and northern pike, but can be distinguished by the markings on their sides, which resemble a chain-link fence. They also have a black, vertical, tear-like bar below the eye. Their bodies are slightly more streamlined and they have a more elongated snout than their relatives. Their deep olive-green color, combined with the chain markings, allow pickerel to blend into the aquatic vegetation where they are most often found.

Chain pickerel are found throughout New England and most of the United States. They are most commonly found in warm, vegetated ponds and small rivers, and tend to lurk in rather shallow water looking for their prey. Their long, slender snout and large mouth are filled with rather large, piercing teeth, enabling them to be voracious feeders. Pickerel prey mostly on smaller fish, but will attack almost anything that moves in the water, including frogs, worms, crayfish, large insects, and even mice. Once they have their prey in their mouth, the inward-pointing teeth move the meal further down the gullet.

Fishermen most often use minnows as live bait to catch chain pickerel, but using frogs or crayfish will catch them as well. Anglers also may use a variety of lures and plugs. Chain pickerel are good fighters and fun to catch. Possibly the biggest challenge is getting the lure or hook out of the mouth without cutting your fingers to shreds. Using pliers and gloves might help. Pickerel remain active in the winter and are sought after by ice fisherman throughout the Northeast. Their white meat is quite tasty but has lots of bones. There are ways to fillet around the bones, but it is not an easy task.

Redfin Pickerel

ESOX AMERICANUS

8–10 inches

I remember fishing as a child in a small brook in the woods near my home in Massachusetts. The brook was very cold and clear with virtually no vegetation. It had a sandy clay bottom with no rocks or gravel. It was a perfect habitat for brook trout and a very safe place for a ten-year-old to spend his summers fishing. Although I was after brook trout, from time to time a small, unusual pickerel would attack my worm as I reeled it in. Even at that early age, I knew that chain pickerel were found in warmer, weedier waters, and this kind did not have the distinctive chain pattern on its sides.

Redfin pickerel are very good looking, with their mottled, green color and narrow dark bands on the sides of their body. Redfin pickerel are quite short and have a proportionally wider girth than chain pickerel. The snout is shorter and broader and they have distinctive red fins. A black, triangular marking below the eye tends to point downward and a bit backward. Like their relatives, chain pickerel and northern pike, redfin pickerel have large mouths for their body size, and rather sharp teeth that point inward. These characteristics make them fierce predators despite their smaller size, usually less than 12 inches in length.

Redfin pickerel tend to frequent the cool, clean water of small streams and small rivers more often than warm, weedy ponds. They hide in the cover of weeds, rocks, or any other debris.

People don't go out fishing for redfin pickerel purposely, as they do for chain pickerel and pike, but like so many other freshwater fish in this area, you may catch one from time to time. If you happen to catch one with a small lure or live bait, you may be surprised by their scrappiness and energy. I am sure people wonder about them as I did as a child.

Northern Pike

ESOX LUCIUS

16–18 inches

Northern pike most closely resemble their relative, chain pickerel, but do not have the chain pattern on their sides. Instead, northern pike have yellowish spots somewhat randomly scattered on their sides. However, the markings of some individuals are similar enough to make identification confusing. Examination of the operculum should solve any confusion: Pike have no scales on the lower half of their operculum, while pickerel have a fully scaled operculum. Other related species include the smaller redfin pickerel and the larger muskellunge. Northern pike have a yellow to white belly.

Pike may be the most aggressive gamefish in the Northeast. They are found in most big rivers and lakes throughout the region. They feed mostly on other fish. They are eating machines, sometimes consuming fish nearly two-thirds their own length. If the fish they swallow is too long to be consumed completely, they will swim around with the tail protruding out of their mouth until the head is digested enough to swallow the remainder of the meal. Their diet also includes ducklings, mice, and even small muskrats.

Pike spawn just after ice-out in the spring and head for weed-filled coves and shallower water than they spent the winter months inhabiting. This can be a great time to fish for pike. They lurk in the shallows just waiting to attack almost anything that moves their way. Pike fishermen commonly use large artificial lures and spinner baits. Surface lures can be very exciting to use as well. Imagine the thrill when you see a wave following your lure seconds before the pike strikes with a vengeance. Live bait, including large shiners, can get results as well. Northern pike may reach 15 pounds or more, particularly in big northeastern rivers such as the Connecticut and the Saint Lawrence.

When fishing for pike, using wire leaders is highly recommended. Their huge mouths and big teeth can shred even the heaviest monofilament lines with ease.

Muskellunge

ESOX MASQUINONGY

25–30 inches

Muskellunge are the largest members of the pike family. They have medium dark bars or blotches on their sides on a background of greenish brown. The general coloration is similar to their relatives, but these markings should not be confused with the chain pickerel's chain-like markings or the northern pike's yellowish spots. Muskellunge also can reach much larger sizes than either of those species. It is not unusual for them to reach lengths well over 35 inches and weights in excess of 30 pounds.

Like their close relatives, the northern pike and the chain pickerel, they are voracious predators. Their streamlined bodies and huge mouths full of large, pointed teeth allow them to devour smaller fish with machine-like efficiency. Muskellunge are at the top of the food chain, feeding mostly on other fish. They tend to prefer soft-finned fish such as suckers and the various species of large minnows. However, they will feed on almost anything they encounter, including small mammals and birds, amphibians, and snakes.

Muskellunge are native to many rivers and lakes throughout the northern half of North America, including large rivers and lakes in the Northeast. They have been introduced into many areas where they previously did not exist. They are less likely to be found in fast-moving rivers, favoring areas where the current slows. They seem to prefer shallow water when they are younger and go deeper as they get older. Muskellunge do well in a wide range of water temperatures, but are found more often in cooler locations. Like other members of the pike family, they are attracted to weeds and debris. Muskellunge actually depend on the presence of weeds for spawning. Their populations have dwindled in some places because of weed removal from the lake bottom near homes and cottages. Because of their ecological role at the top of the food chain, and because they require relatively large feeding territories, muskellunge are not abundant and may be difficult to find. They have well-defined territories within a lake or river, and although they will roam within that defined area, they don't tend to leave it.

Wire leaders and 30-pound test line are recommended to withstand their large teeth. With patience and persistence, any large lure, crankbait, spinner, or spoon might hook one. Many fishermen prefer using large, live baitfish. Just toss it out among some weeds or log debris or near a drop-off, and wait for the lurking predator to attack your bait.

Sea Lamprey

PETROMYZON MARINUS

24–30 inches

From a chronological standpoint, sea lamprey should have been the first fish in this book instead of the last. They are from the most primitive class of fish, even more primitive than sharks, skates, and rays. Sea lamprey have no true jaws, but only a disk-shaped mouth. Their skeletons have no bones and are made up of cartilage. Lamprey are classified as vertebrates, but they have only a cartilage notochord, the precursor to a backbone. They are eel-like in appearance, and at a glance might be confused with American eels. A closer look would show several big differences. Sea lampreys have seven pairs of gill pouches where water goes in and is puffed back out. They have only a single nostril. Sea lampreys have no pelvic or pectoral fins. They have two flimsy, little dorsal fins and a caudal fin. They are olive-brown to silvery grey, with a white belly. They have scaleless, smooth-looking skin.

Sea lamprey are naturally anadromous fish and wouldn't be of major consequence if they hadn't entered the Great Lakes and Lake Champlain, where they have become landlocked. Canals built to allow ships to get from the Saint Lawrence River to the Great Lakes connected the ocean to the Great Lakes and allowed sea lamprey to make their way there and become established. They have become an invasive species that parasitizes freshwater fish that are not adapted to deal with this intruder. Thus, they have greatly affected populations of fish such as lake trout (and other trout species), salmon, walleye, whitefish, burbot, and catfish.

Sea lamprey first attach themselves to the side of a fish using strong suction with their disk-shaped mouth. Using their rows of rasping teeth and scraping tongue, they puncture and digest their way through the fish's skin and feed mostly on the body fluids. They are not a very good parasite, in the sense that they most often kill their host rather than just stealing nourishment and sending it on its way. Fishermen in the Great Lakes and Lake Champlain occasionally catch salmon, trout, and other species with round scars on their sides, evidence that these fish escaped the grip of this menacing parasite.

Many efforts have been made to control sea lamprey populations. Traps are set in the rivers and streams that the adults swim up to spawn. Lampricides are used to kill the larvae while they are still in their pre-parasitic stage. These poisons are selective and don't harm other species. Studies have shown that these efforts have controlled sea lamprey populations in the Great Lakes and Lake Champlain.

Glossary of Fish Terminology

adipose fin
Small, soft fin located on the dorsal surface of some fish, including trout, salmon, and catfish.

air bladder
Air-filled sac in the body cavity of a fish that allows the fish to remain the same density as the water no matter its depth.

anadromous fish
Ocean-dwelling fish that migrate up freshwater rivers and streams to spawn.

anal fin
Single, keel-like fin on the ventral surface of a fish, behind the anus.

anterior
The front or toward the front.

barbel
Fleshy, string-like structure found near the mouth on some fish, such as the "whiskers" on a catfish.

catadromous fish
Freshwater fish that migrate to the ocean to spawn.

caudal fin
Tail fin.

countershading
A form of protective coloration whereby a fish is darkest on its dorsal surface, lightest on its ventral surface, and intermediately shaded in the middle to blend into the background. Also known as Thayer's Law.

dorsal
Upper surface of a fish.

dorsal fin
Large fin on the dorsal surface (sometimes can be doubled with rays and/or spines).

family
Scientific grouping more inclusive than genus.

fry
Young fish.

gill rakers
  Rake-like projections on the gill arches of a fish that are used to strain out debris and keep it from harming the gill filaments.

larvae
  Immature stage of life in some animals.

lateral line
  Unique sense organ found in fish used to detect motion and vibrations. It is usually a visible line running horizontally along the mid-lateral sides of a fish.

nymph
  Immature stage of life in some insects (incomplete metamorphosis).

opercular flap
  Flap of tissue on the posterior margin of the operculum.

operculum
  Gill cover.

paired fins
  The pectoral and pelvic fins on a fish.

pectoral fins
  Anterior-most paired fins on a fish.

pelvic fins
  Posterior-most paired fins on a fish.

posterior
  The rear or toward the rear.

semi-anadromous fish
  Estuarine-dwelling fish that spawn in freshwater.

spawn
  To lay eggs.

tail
  Narrow, fleshy posterior end where the caudal fin connects to the fish.

ventral
  Lower belly surface of a fish.

References and Recommended Reading

Berra, Tim M. *Freshwater Fish Distribution*. Chicago: University of Chicago Press, 2001.

Burr, L. M., and B. M. Burr. *A Field Guide to Freshwater Fishes: North America North of Mexico*. Peterson Field Guide Series. New York: Houghton Mifflin, 1991.

Fishes of Maine. Augusta: Maine Department of Inland Fisheries and Wildlife, 2002. Available at http://www.maine.gov/ifw/fishing/pdfs/fishesofmaine.pdf.

McClane, A. J. *McClane's Field Guide to Freshwater Fish of North America*. New York: Henry Holt, 1978.

Mugford, Paul S. *Illustrated Manual of Massachusetts Freshwater Fishes*. Boston: Massachusetts Division of Fisheries and Game, 1969.

Prosek, James. *Trout: An Illustrated History*. New York: Alfred A. Knopf, 1997.

Reid, George K. *Pond Life*. Illustrated by Sally D. Kaicher and Tom Dolan. New York: St. Martin's Press, 2001.

Scarola, John F. *Freshwater Fishes of New Hampshire*. Concord: New Hampshire Fish and Game Department Division of Inland Fisheries, 1987.

Schultz, Ken. *Ken Schultz's Field Guide to Freshwater Fish*. Hoboken, N.J.: Wiley & Sons, 2004.

Scott, W. B., and E. J. Crossman. *Freshwater Fishes of Canada*. Ottawa: Fisheries Research Board of Canada, 1973.

Smith, C. Lavett. *The Inland Fishes of New York State*. Albany: New York State Department of Environmental Conservation, 1985.

Smith, Robert H. *Native Trout of North America*. Illustrated by Howard G. Hughes. Portland, Ore.: Frank Amato Publications, 1984.

Steinberg, Dick. *The Complete Freshwater Fisherman*. New York: Prentice Hall, 1987.

———. *Freshwater Gamefish of North America*. New York: Prentice Hall, 1987.

Sternberg, Dick, and Bill Ignizio. *Panfish*. The Hunting and Fishing Library. Minnetonka, Minn.: Cy DeCosse, 1987.

Wood, Ian, ed. *The Dorling Kindersley Encyclopedia of Fishing: The Complete Guide to the Fish, Tackle, and Techniques of Fresh and Saltwater Angling*. New York: Dorling Kindersley, Inc., 1994.

Zim, Herbert S., and Hurst H. Shoemaker. *Fishes: A Guide to Fresh and Salt-Water Species*. Illustrated by James Gordon Irving. New York: Simon and Schuster, 1956.

Suggested Web Sites

Connecticut Department of
Environmental Protection
  http://www.ct.gov/dep/site/default.asp

Maine Department of Inland Fisheries
and Wildlife
  http://www.maine.gov/ifw/fishing/
  index.htm

Massachusetts Division of Fisheries
and Wildlife
  http://www.mass.gov/dfwele/dfw

New Hampshire Fish and Game
Department
  http://www.wildlife.state.nh.us/

New York Department of Environmental
Conservation
  http://www.dec.ny.gov/outdoor/
  fishing.html

Pennsylvania Fish and Boat Commission
  http://www.fish.state.pa.us/fishin1.htm

Rhode Island Department of
Environmental Management
  http://www.dem.ri.gov/topics/
  fwtopics.htm

Vermont Fish and Wildlife Department
  http://www.vtfishandwildlife.com/
  fisheries_list.cfm